How to
Resolve Conflict

About the Peace and Security in the 21st Century Series

Until recently, security was defined mostly in geopolitical terms with the assumption that it could only be achieved through at least the threat of military force. Today, however, people from as different backgrounds as planners in the Pentagon and veteran peace activists think in terms of human or global security, where no one is secure unless everyone is secure in all areas of their lives. This means that it is impossible nowadays to separate issues of war and peace, the environment, sustainability, identity, global health, and the like.

The books in this series aim to make sense of this changing world of peace and security by investigating security issues and peace efforts that involve cooperation at several levels. By looking at how security and peace interrelate at various stages of conflict, the series explores new ideas for a fast-changing world and seeks to redefine and rethink what peace and security mean in the first decades of the new century.

Multidisciplinary in approach and authorship, the books cover a variety of topics, focusing on the overarching theme that students, scholars, practitioners, and policymakers have to find new models and theories to account for, diagnose, and respond to the difficulties of a more complex world. Authors are established scholars and practitioners in their fields of expertise.

In addition, it is hoped that the series will contribute to bringing together authors and readers in concrete, applied projects, and thus help create, under the sponsorship of Alliance for Peacebuilding (AfP), a community of practice. The series is sponsored by the Alliance for Peacebuilding, and edited by Charles Hauss, government liaison. http://www.allianceforpeacebuilding.org

To view all titles in the series, please visit:

https://rowman.com/Action/SERIES/RL/RLPS21

Or scan:

How to Resolve Conflict

A Practical Mediation Manual

By James E. Gilman

ROWMAN & LITTLEFIELD
Lanham • Boulder • New York • London

Published by Rowman & Littlefield
A wholly owned subsidiary of The Rowman & Littlefield Publishing Group, Inc.
4501 Forbes Boulevard, Suite 200, Lanham, Maryland 20706
www.rowman.com

Unit A, Whitacre Mews, 26-34 Stannary Street, London SE11 4AB

British Library Cataloguing in Publication Information Available

Library of Congress Cataloging-in-Publication Data Available

ISBN 978-1-4422-6796-1 (cloth : alk. paper)
ISBN 978-1-4422-6797-8 (pbk. : alk. paper)
ISBN 978-1-4422-6798-5 (electronic)

∞™ The paper used in this publication meets the minimum requirements of American National Standard for Information Sciences—Permanence of Paper for Printed Library Materials, ANSI/NISO Z39.48-1992.

Printed in the United States of America

Dedicated to

Fairfield Mediation Center
Harrisonburg, Virginia

Contents

Contents

Preface and Acknowledgments

Mediation is a form of dispute resolution rooted in ancient virtues of character and civility. Although sometimes forgotten and sometimes neglected, it nevertheless persists and sometimes today flourishes as a collaborative alternative to more adversarial forms of dispute resolution. Mediation is also a discipline; it consists of a certain set of interpersonal communication and problem-solving skills that can be learned and practiced. As a "how to" manual, this book aims to provide the practical materials needed to cultivate these skills and the capacity to succeed as a mediator. Completing this course of study and mastering these skills, however, does not officially certify one as a mediator. Certification is the prerogative of the supreme courts of the various states and provinces; they establish criteria and supervise the training and certification of mediators. Although this manual provides most of the materials necessary for certification, more in-depth study of various areas of expertise (e.g., family/domestic mediation; business mediation) is necessary to meet the requirements of certification. For example, a prospective mediator must study the regional guidelines and policies regarding divorce, and complete a series of observations as well as an internship under the guidance of a certified mediator. Nevertheless, this handbook provides much of the material needed for preparing one to be certified as a mediator.

This book is intended as a teaching/training manual. It does not attempt to analyze and critique the extensive scholarly literature on this subject, although the results of some of that research are included. One difficulty that emerges from reading scholarly literature is the proliferation of terms and concepts that are employed in writing about mediation and conflict resolution. Questions are unavoidable: What constitutes a "conflict"? What traits characterize a "resolution"? How do we know when a conflict is resolved?

Do "mediation" and "negotiation" refer to a process or do they refer to substantive beliefs about the prospects for human relationships, or both? Other terms appear in this book that bear a great deal of baggage—peace, peacebuilding, peacemaking, transformation, transformative, and so on. For example, What exactly is transformed? An issue, a relationship, a perspective? And how do we know when conflict has been successfully resolved or transformed?

I do not try to answer all of these questions, although in the course of the text some of them are addressed and answered. There are, however, a few clarifications that might be helpful. What the adjectival use of the term "conflict" should properly qualify is somewhat controversial. Does mediation entail "conflict resolution," "conflict management," or "conflict transformation?" Or all three? John Lederach insists that "conflict transformation" is the preferable phrase, because it captures more fully and clearly the nature and character of conflict as a phenomenon of human relationships.[1] He rejects "conflict resolution" because it implies that conflict itself is bad, is temporary, and can be terminated rather quickly. "Conflict management" is an improvement, he argues, insofar as it suggests that conflict is ongoing and requires a prolonged process. But "management" is misleading insofar as it suggests that people can and should be manipulated or relationships controlled. "Conflict transformation" is the preferred phrase, insists Lederach, partly because it more nearly reflects the fact that "conflict" is not necessarily bad, that it is more or less "permanent" in human relationships, and that mediation does not attempt to control people. Indeed, "conflict" is "dialectical," he argues; not only do human relationships generate conflict, but that very conflict itself generates conditions that in turn change or "transform" those same human relationships. Left alone, conflict may be destructive; but by engaging it, conflict may very well be altered and transformed, albeit not entirely resolved or eliminated.

Robert Bush and Joseph Folger, in *The Promise of Mediation: The Transformative Approach to Mediation* (2004), similarly argue for mediation as primarily a process for transforming relationships instead of simply a process of resolving a set of issues. Mediation understood as primarily a problem-solving process attempts to get disputants to mutually agree to solutions to certain concrete contentious issues, and in doing so achieves no more than a short-term truce between parties. Like Lederach, they insist that much more than problem-solving can and should be expected of mediation. Mediation has the power to go beyond problem-solving to a deeper social, interpersonal level, such that profound, permanent transformative changes in relationships are possible. Bush and Folger argue that mediation can promise these more durable changes for two reasons: first, because mediation "empowers," encouraging disputants to shape their own issues as they wish and discover and agree to solutions that are of their own making; and secondly, because mediation enables all parties to "recognize" other disputants, by helping them understand the other's issues and motives and needs.

Consistent with this "promise" (that mediation is capable, beyond problem-solving, of transforming relationships) is the mission of the Arbinger Institute. This Institute focuses on the role of mediation in training leaders. It employs phrases like "conflict resolution," "peacemaking," "peacebuilding," and "anatomy of peace."[2] In training leaders, the Institute promotes a Peacemaking Pyramid that sets forth conflict resolution as a dynamic process in which disputants not only problem-solve issues but investigate progressively deeper levels of relationships, personal and professional. Each descending level not only makes possible a fuller resolution to the conflict but also builds a stronger relationship among those people involved in the dispute. This approach involves "peacemaking" in that it addresses not only behavior but the motives and needs that drive behavior. As a result of progressing through these levels of conflict and of addressing motives and needs, a foundation begins to build for enduring peaceful relationships; accordingly, not only are immediate issues resolved, but future conflicts are either prevented or more easily transformed into occasions for constructive, collaborative projects. Assuming a substantial peacebuilding process such as this, it makes sense to speak not only about conflict transformation, as does Lederach, but also of an "anatomy of peace" that includes conflict resolution and management: "resolution" because although perhaps not "bad" in itself conflict can be destructive if motives and needs are not addressed; and "management" because it is not people who are managed and controlled but levels of a dynamic process, on which more durable relationships can be built.

A classic book exemplifying the "best practices" for these various mediation strategies, from conflict transformation to peacebuilding, is *The Mediator's Handbook* by Beer, Packard, and Stief. It provides tools, frameworks, and strategies that help people and neutrals work through levels of issues, motives, and needs. It also provides language and phrases helpful to neutrals in progressing through the various stages of the mediation process and levels of issues, motives, and needs. This book aspires to incorporate some of these "best practices"; it promotes mediation as a process capable not only of short-term problem-solving but also capable of transforming more profoundly and permanently the character of relationships. My own experience as a neutral suggests that although mediation has the power to resolve disputes at a variety of levels (problem-solve issues, cultivate communication skills, transform relationships, build peace), each mediated case is unique. In some cases, little more than problem-solving issues is accomplished; in other cases, more profound levels of transformation are possible—restructuring and healing relationships.

How to Resolve Conflict: A Practical Mediation Manual harvests the fruit of these scholarly works along with a couple decades of experience volunteering as a mediator with Fairfield Mediation Center in Harrisonburg, Virginia, and of teaching a course, "Mediation: Theory and Practice," at Mary Baldwin University. Its strengths, such as they are, result from interacting with disputants, and with many colleagues and students, all of whom contributed constructively and critically. Especially I would like to acknowledge Timothy Ruebke, Executive Director of Fairfield Center, Nicole Kennedy (student assistant), colleagues in the Department of Philosophy and Religion at Mary Baldwin University, Roderic Owen, Andrea Cornett-Scott, Edward Scott, Pat Hunt, Katherine Low, Kenneth Beals, and colleagues Robert Everett, Jack Hill, and Tom O'Conner. I would also like to acknowledge others with whom I interacted significantly regarding conflict and mediation, including Perry Neel, John Hooe, Susan Read, Eric Laurenzo, John Wilkerson, Susan Peyton, Thomas Howell, John Lane, Paul Nancarrow, Shelby Owen, Dawn Frankfurt, Catherine Riordan, Mark Kersey, John Kiger, "Scottie" Scott, Matt Gaffney, Bernard J. Moore, and Dave Baker; and not least of all supportive members of my family, children Ian and Caitrin, and siblings Roger, Dan, Randy, Joyce, and Melodie, all of whom practice mediation values.

Finally, I owe a great debt of gratitude to Marie-Claire Antoine, Senior Acquisitions Editor at Rowman & Littlefield, Monica Savaglia, Assistant Editor, and anonymous reviewers whose critical comments and suggestions improved the quality of this book.

NOTES

1. See John Paul Lederach's book *Building Peace: Sustainable Reconciliation in Divided Societies*. Washington, DC: United States Institute of Peace (1998), Chapter One for an elaboration on this discussion. See also the article "Conflict Transformation and Peacemaking," http://www.colorado.edu/conflict/transform/jpall.htm, or Heidi Burgess & Guy Burgess, Co-directors, Conflict Research Consortium, University of Colorado, at burgess@colorado.edu.

2. See such books as *Leadership and Self-Deception* (2002) and *The Anatomy of Peace* (2008) published by the Arbinger Institute, for an elaboration of these key phrases.

I

THEORY

1

Theories of Conflict Resolution

MODELS FOR RESOLVING CONFLICTS

The ability to resolve conflict is perhaps the most practical life skill a person can cultivate and exercise. Few days pass wherein a person does not encounter tensions, disagreement, discord, dissension, and conflict of some sort and intensity. Humans commonly encounter conflicts as members of a family, as co-workers and professionals, as students, roommates, lovers, spouses, friends, patrons, consumers, colleagues, athletes, coaches, neighbors; indeed, as human beings. It seems as if tension and conflict partly define what it means to be human and to live in relation to other humans.

It is helpful, accordingly, to identify various conceptual frameworks within which humans often situate themselves for resolving conflicts. Each framework provides a unique perspective for interpreting and resolving conflict; each has its secular and religious versions; each has strengths and weaknesses. Consider three general, competing models of conflict resolution: Domination, Prevention, and Transformation, the latter of which is most conducive to mediating conflicts. For each approach I briefly discuss (1) aim, (2) means for achieving that aim, and (3) assessment.

Domination Model[1]

The Domination approach aims at guaranteeing stability and security by subduing and suppressing opposition and conflict, by establishing a clear and acknowledged authority that is able with superior strength to enforce order and sustain stability. As the most common approach to resolving conflict, the Domination Model presupposes that conflict is mostly bad and harmful and represents a defective, corrupting force in society that is best suppressed, banished, outlawed. Established authority aims at stability and order, and does so by "laying down the law" and enforcing it with superior force. Indeed, the aim of stability justifies, at least for some Domination authorities, the use of almost any means necessary to secure it.

The ordinary means for securing stability, via this model, include measures both affirmative/positive and measures antagonistic/negative. Positives include clear and common laws and their enforcement according to public procedures and due process. A fair and just system of rewards and punishments, benefits and burdens, is crucial for achieving order and stability. Negatives include measures calculated to elicit compliance motivated largely by fear: threats and intimidation; measures that coerce, compel, constrain, control, even bully and deprive by use of violence, abuse, and torture. This model, no doubt, is the one most commonly employed by all forms of governments, from tyrannical to democratic. In addition, it frames the way a wide variety of social and political communities operate, including families; churches; local, state, and international corporations; athletics; universities; cults; and so on.

The Domination Model's approach to conflict resolution is familiar and common, represented, for example, by the Reagan administration, which in 1982 referred to the MX missile as a "peacemaker" or "peacekeeper"; a weapon of mass destruction calculated to intimidate and threaten opponents in order to defer and suppress conflict. This model commonly dominates the way nations deal with tensions and conflicts internally and externally: the United States with its massive military budget, and Russia, China, the European Union, and Middle Eastern nations all operate largely within the framework of the Domination Model. As we shall see below, the criminal justice systems in these nations also presuppose the Domination Model. Furthermore, in personal relationships this model is sometimes used by families: by spouses in relating to each other and by parents in raising children; fear and intimidation, sometimes in the form of abusive language and even violence, are used to establish order and stability.

How would you assess this model, its aim and procedures for resolving conflict? No doubt creating an orderly and stable society is desirable and compelling. A society without clear laws and governmental authority undermines its capacity to provide the resources and values needed to function in a civilized way. This model, however, is readily susceptible to habits of misusing and abusing its superior strength, both against its own citizens as well as against other nations. It often is so consumed with subduing and suppressing conflict, with maintaining dominance and institutionalizing structures of force and violence, that a society's entire political and economic life pivots around it. Thus, when conflicts arise adherents of the Domination Model instinctively resort to superior force for subduing conflict and for establishing social order. In being so preoccupied it often fails to pursue alternative, more advanced, civilized ways of resolving conflicts, securing stability, and seeking peace.

Prevention Model[2]

A less common approach to resolving conflict aims at pre-empting conflict, either externally by preventing it from arising in the first place, or internally by preventing it from affecting one's inner tranquility, or both. Like the Domination approach, this model presupposes that conflict is bad and harmful and that resources should be marshaled not in order to suppress or bury conflict but in order to eliminate or avoid somehow conditions that give rise to conflict in the first place, conditions that prevent it from taking root at all.

The means for pre-empting and preventing conflict externally entails establishing conditions of equality and harmony that tend to preclude tensions from emerging in the first place: for example, cultivating a common, communal character of mutuality and equality, of cooperation and consensus, of calm tranquility. The means for preventing conflict internally entails habits of self-control and discipline, of reflection and emotional self-sufficiency that, in spite of external distractions, favor inner calm and tranquility.

Some families, businesses, and communities strive to emulate this model of conflict resolution. Collectives and co-ops fashion themselves after this model. They intentionally establish a kind of corporate ethos of tranquility based on principles of harmony and cooperation, on policies of mutuality and responsibility, and on a model for the equal distribution of authority and power. Usually such communities include policies not only of procedural justice and freedom but also of egalitarian economic outcomes. Intentional monastic communities include the Benedictines and Franciscans, where virtues of humility, repentance, forgiveness, tolerance, silence, and love create external and internal conditions that tend to minimize tensions and conflicts. Other communes exemplifying this Prevention Model, like the Shakers, advocate an approach in which the equality of men and women (equal status and equal leadership roles) establishes conditions that minimize if not pre-empt the possibility of conflict.

How would you assess this model, its strengths and weaknesses? To some extent most people desire to prevent and avoid unnecessary conflict, although there are exceptions. They try to create a style of personal and professional life that reduces tension as much as possible and averts discord. Studies show that reducing tension is healthy for individuals as well as for societies; it enhances the quality of life. But this model of peacemaking is somewhat unrealistic for all but small, strictly intentional communities; it tends to ignore the fact that conflict is to some extent an unavoidable dimension of human interaction and one that humans should face up to and not always try to prevent. Its perception that tensions and conflicts can mostly be avoided is misguided; they will not go away. Humans and societies would be better off facing up to conflict and finding ways of resolving instead of dodging it.

Transformation Model[3]

The approach for resolving conflict that is most favorable to mediation is the Transformation Model. What is most distinctive to this model, and most unlike the previous two, is its forthright and candid acceptance of conflict as a normal and common dimension of human experience. It presupposes that conflict and controversy are not necessarily destructive and bad, to be suppressed or avoided. Instead, often they are occasions for constructive rapprochement and reconciliation. This model aims, accordingly, at transforming tension and conflict, alienation and discord, into occasions for constructive communication, collaboration, and cooperation. No doubt some conflicts seem so daunting and deeply rooted that transformation is difficult. This model presupposes that most conflicts can nevertheless be transformed and resolved peacefully.

This model equates "peace" and "peacemaking" with the ability to creatively transform conflict by finding resolutions satisfactory to all. The means for accomplishing such transformation entails a peacemaking process of non-coercive, non-violent restructuring of relationships, so that power imbalances are addressed and collaborative solutions emerge, resolutions that all parties contribute to and benefit from. I develop the values and principles of this model more fully in chapter 3, and only mention them briefly here. The Transformation Model (1) discovers the root causes of conflict, (2) establishes common ground among disputants, (3) guarantees a fair and just process of communication, (4) restructures power imbalances in the relationship, and (5) requires the use of certain communication skills so that disputants hear each other and respond constructively. What results very often in mediation is peacebuilding on various levels: the resolution of certain issues; the transformation and healing of interpersonal tensions; a foundation for communication and constructive relationships.

Examples of the Transformation Model are fairly common these days. Negotiation and mediation are an important part of international diplomacy. The United Nations frequently tries to get nations to resolve disputes peacefully through negotiation or through the use of the mediation services it provides. Gandhi, Dr. King, and the Truth and Reconciliation Commission in South Africa (Nelson Mandela and Bishop Tutu) successfully employed the Transformation Model for dealing with profound and deeply rooted structural injustices. More locally, parties involved in labor disputes often make use of mediators when negotiations fail to achieve a resolution. Some corporations and families beneficially employ mediation as a primary approach to easing community tensions and resolving interpersonal disputes.

How would you assess the Transformation Model? In very many contexts—global, professional, and personal—tensions and conflicts can successfully be resolved employing the Transformation Model. Studies show that its methodology is consistently and reliably successful at resolving disagreements and conflicts and at averting violence and warfare. However, this model requires discipline, skill, time, energy, and voluntary participation, features that are not always immediately available in all situations, as when direct and aggressive self-defense is necessary. This fact, however, should not detract from the reality that intentional and skilled habits of mediation, if given the chance, can successfully transform many conflicts into creative solutions, in sometimes surprising ways.

RETRIBUTIVE AND RESTORATIVE JUSTICE

The criminal justice system is an all too familiar dimension of everyday life in most societies. Media outlets not only flood markets with stories of crime and punishment but also promote documentaries of criminals and the criminal justice system itself. Criminals, jails, prisons, forensics, police, investigators, courts, witnesses, prosecutors, judges, juries, and so on—are often news. Societies spend significant tax monies on building courthouses and prisons and correctional institutions, on food and clothing, on judges and wardens and staff to accommodate crime and criminals; it is big business. Criminal Justice is one of the popular majors at colleges and universities; not surprisingly, for crime is a constant and pervasive part of human life. We lock doors and secure homes and vehicles and neighborhoods without much thought, knowing that we too at any time could be victims. How a society views and treats crime and criminals is an important social barometer of its preferred model for dispute resolution. Today there are at least two major justice traditions for treating crime—retributive and restorative. The former is the system most are familiar with; the latter is a more recent, less familiar complementary system.

What is distinctive to a retributive system is the *relationship* with which it occupies itself; its focus is on the relationship between the criminal and the state and the state's laws. Crime is primarily treated as a violation of laws and an offense against the state. The primary damage inflicted by crime is presumed to be against an institution, and not a person(s). The criminal, therefore, should be appropriately and justly punished by that institution, whether local, state, federal, or international. The purpose of the criminal justice system is to determine through its courts the appropriate blame and just punishment for those who are guilty. Generally, it is thought that just punishment should "fit" the crime; that it should be fair and equal to the offense committed. Fair and equal is sometimes considered to be a punishment severe enough to persuade the criminal not to commit the crime again. In any case, fair, retributive justice is the appropriate response to any offense against the state and its laws. Retributive justice is clearly a function of the Domination Model and presupposes its values and way of resolving conflicts.

In contrast to retributive, restorative justice is a less familiar alternative that focuses primarily on the *relationship* between criminal and victim. It presupposes the values of the Transformation Model and acknowledges that the core of crime is not the damage inflicted on the laws of the state but on the lives of victims, of people and communities. The aim of restorative justice, accordingly, is to repair precisely that relationship; to transform the relationship between criminal and victim from one of violence, alienation, hostility, and suspicion to one of mutual trust, respect, and peacemaking. Of course several conditions must be met in order for restorative justice to take place. First, both criminal and victim must voluntarily participate in a process of mediation. This choice is perhaps more difficult for the victim than for the criminal. Secondly, the victim of crime is never merely a single individual but is always also a neighborhood and community. Therefore, community representatives—business leaders, ministers, social workers, neighbors—are usually involved along with the person(s) directly victimized by crime. Thirdly, a fair and just restorative response to crime is not to punish the criminal so much as to work out an agreement through the mediation process, an agreement between criminal and victim/community. This means that both victim and criminal are empowered to work out a constructive plan for rehabilitating and restoring the relationship between the criminal and community. With the help of mediation and a neutral, both are involved in restructuring the relationship in a way that enhances mutual understanding and service of each to the other. Some form of community service is common, in which the offender serves the community in a designated capacity that helps restore the relationship with persons victimized. Restorative justice is clearly a function of the Transformation Model of peacemaking. As a creative, alternative version of justice it addresses relationships and needs and interests not addressed by retributive systems.

Some advocates of restorative justice promote it is a model that should displace and replace entirely systems of retributive justice. Others argue, as I do, that restorative justice should expand and supplement the retributive system, even though at times restorative programs may very well replace retributive approaches and penalties. Especially for juvenile delinquents, restorative programs, aided by a mediator, aim to repair a broken relationship with the community in order to reduce rates of recidivism. It does so by minimizing the length of incarceration and maximizing community service under the guidance of a mentor. The difference in aim and method between these two models is obvious. Retribution addresses the relationship between criminal and state, whereas restoration addresses the relationship between criminal and victimized community. Retribution employs punitive measures to secure justice, restorative employs regenerative, conciliatory measures to rehabilitate a relationship. The former focuses on an individual, the latter on a community; the former is legal, the latter social; the former focuses on procedural justice (i.e., fair punishment), the latter on egalitarian justice (i.e., social rehabilitation and community reconciliation); the former tends to be reflexive, the latter transformative. Accordingly, restorative justice partners with mediation for the purpose not only of problem-solving, but for peace-building, for building into the offender's character and interpersonal relationships a way of communicating and interacting with others that is civil and constructive and enduring. Chapter 9 further investigates the application of mediation and restorative justice to criminal justice systems.

INQUIRY AND REFLECTION EXERCISES

1. In a paragraph, describe and explain a conflict you have recently experienced. What are the important issues at stake in the conflict? Were you able to resolve the conflict? How or why not?

2. The way families treat conflict and peacemaking tends toward one or the other of the three models of peacemaking. Discuss the tendency toward one or two of these models as practiced in your own family.

3. After the terrorist attack of 9/11 (2001), the United States responded by undertaking two wars, first in Afghanistan and then in Iraq. In doing so it was implementing the Domination Model of peacemaking, by showing superior strength through conventional military engagement. But suppose the United States instead implemented the Transformation Model of peacemaking. What would its response to 9/11 "look like" in that case?

4. Online, access a restorative justice organization or program in your home community. Print off two or three pages. Describe in a typed page or two how this organization understands restorative justice, its goals and objectives, and how it achieves those goals.

NOTES

1. This model is familiar to historians as *pax Romana*. This model was perfected by ancient Roman emperors from Augustus to Aurelius and co-opted by Christianity beginning with the Emperor Constantine.

2. This model is sometimes referred to as *pax Tranquillitatis,* and historically is represented by monastic communities, like the Franciscans and communes that followed the teachings of Tolstoy, such as the Life and Labor Commune in Russia and the Christian Commonwealth Colony in Georgia, the United States.

3. In the Western tradition the Transformation Model has its roots in *pax Christi*, referring to the majority pacifist tendencies of Christians in the early few centuries of the Common Era. This peacemaking habit of early Christians became marginalized when the Emperor Constantine converted and began reshaping Christianity to the Roman Empire's Domination Model.

2

Mediation: Values and Principles

VARIETIES OF CONFLICT RESOLUTION

Conflict seems to be an unavoidable dimension of human interaction. Routine, daily conflicts arise and are often resolved unofficially and interpersonally. Through informal conversation and bargaining tensions are diffused and conflicts successfully settled. But sometimes in trying to resolve interpersonal conflicts, whether at home or work or play, people take matters into their own hands, resorting to threats, intimidation and coercion, even violence; for example, fear of being fired from a job or punished for breaking a law often causes further tension and conflict; or, growing up in families, most of us have experienced to some degree the fear generated by threats of harm and punishment delivered by parents, hoping to maintain domestic order.

One service civil society can provide its citizens is orderly, reliable ways for resolving conflicts. Advanced societies provide a variety of options, most commonly litigation. But other options are generally available, such as negotiation, arbitration, and mediation. Our focus is on mediation, but it is helpful to place it in the context of other official forums for resolving conflicts (see figure 2.1).

Litigation

The most familiar official format for resolving conflict is the judicial or court system. Neighbors file a complaint over a constantly barking dog and rely on a local justice system to fairly adjudicate and satisfy their complaint. Disputants often depend on litigation, on a just, due process for resolving conflict. They retain an attorney or legal counsel who is not neutral but who advocates on behalf of one particular party to the dispute. The counselor represents his/her

Figure 2.1.   Continuum from Most to Least Hierarchical

client before a third party, the law/court, and seeks to persuade the court to
rule in favor of the client. The disputants may testify and hear testimony and
otherwise make their case in hope that those with power—the law, the court, a
judge, or jury—will rule favorably. What is distinct to litigation is that a third
party—the law, a judge, or jury, not the disputants—retains the power to adjudicate the case, to decide what a fair and just outcome shall be. Many people
are familiar with court cases and trials, but most litigated disputes and cases
are settled "on the courthouse steps," before trial, as plea bargains.

Arbitration

Like litigation, arbitration relies on a third party for resolving conflicts and
like litigation the arbitrator retains the power to deliberate and make a final
decision regarding the disposition and outcome of the case. Like mediation
the arbitrator is a third party neutral; but unlike mediation arbitration "is a
more formal process . . . the arbitrator holds a hearing, listens to testimony and
evidence . . . and," as in litigation, "makes a reward."[1] Often an arbitrator is
appointed to a case by the court as an expert in a particular field, such as issues
related to business transactions or landlord/tenant relations. Like mediation,
arbitration may employ shuttle diplomacy and like mediation it may take place
as an extension of the court system or undertaken as a private sector service.

Mediation (see page 13)

Facilitation

Facilitation is a process outside the legal system that aims at designing and
coordinating meetings. It takes place most commonly in the business and
corporate world as an organizational tool for efficiently accomplishing collective goals and objectives. It involves a neutral third party whose goal is to
guarantee that meetings "stay on task," and that the conversation and delib-
erations are civil, fair, and productive. The facilitator does not lead the group
or meeting, but possesses a set of skills by which she is able to actively guide
participants toward collaboration and consensus. The facilitator is impartial,
like a mediator, but not in control of specific stages of a mediation process.

Negotiation

Although negotiation is a formal and official method for resolving conflicts,
it is also the most common informal means by which people resolve conflicts.

Daily people face each other directly and converse, bargain, confer, dicker, haggle, and compromise in order to come to some agreement regarding issues that are to some degree important to them. More formally, negotiation refers to a venue in which parties, who share interests, discuss directly among themselves issues about which they disagree and for which they desire resolution. What is distinct about negotiation is that no third party facilitates the conversation and bargaining; and most importantly decision-making power remains with the parties in dispute, not some third party. Familiar to many people are cases in which employer and representatives of employees periodically negotiate and update labor contracts, wages, promotions, and benefits. Many principles and values constituting negotiation also are essential for successful mediation; indeed, neutrals encourage disputants to negotiate between themselves in working toward agreement.

MEDIATION: VALUES AND PRINCIPLES

The focus of this handbook is the process and practice of mediation, as an increasingly common alternative means of resolving conflict. Over the years, this approach has proven itself to be successful. "Research suggests that once the disputants have agreed to mediate, there is an excellent chance that they can reach agreement. One study reports a 94 percent agreement rate (Clarke, Valente, & Mace, 1992)."[2] A basic definition of mediation can be put simply: *it is a process in which a neutral third party helps two or more parties come to their own resolutions to conflicts they are having over one or more issues.* If you were to comment on this definition, what elements in it would you highlight? At least three elements, in my view, should be accented.

First, mediation is a process. There is no magic formula by which conflicts are resolved. But there is a process of several stages that, if followed closely, tends to place the disputants in a position of equality that makes it likely they will resolve many of their issues, and perhaps even transform their relationship. These stages are labeled variously by mediators. The labels I use are:

- Stage One: Opening Statement
- Stage Two: Story-Telling
- Stage Three: Clarification
- Stage Four: Negotiation
- Stage Five: Agreement

In Part II, each of these steps will be discussed and explained at some length. For now, it is helpful to note that successful mediation entails a deliberate, intentional process that a neutral is responsible for; by shepherding the mediation through these stages, resolution is a likely outcome. In a sense, then, the mediator as facilitator is an advocate for a process and a fair outcome, and not an advocate for the position of either one of the disputants. Put another way, the power of the neutral as facilitator guarantees that each stage of the mediation process is successfully completed and that the outcome, the agreement, is fair.

Secondly, a mediator not only advocates for a process but, as a third party facilitator, remains neutral and impartial. As a neutral the mediator does not play the role of advocate for one party or the other, as does a lawyer; instead the mediator remains impartial and objective in relation to the interests and desires and needs of the disputants. The mediator aims to establish a context in which the parties in dispute can negotiate solutions to conflicts, with the assistance of a third party neutral. However, the neutral is an advocate for a process, procedural steps by which the interests of all parties are addressed and resolved; accordingly, as a neutral the mediator does not and cannot advocate on behalf of the self-interest of any of the disputants. Samuel Forlenza describes this twofold role of the neutral: "The mediator is a conflict manager and a resolution facilitator."[3] That said, it is common for neutrals, during the process of a mediation session, to feel drawn to and sympathize with one of the disputants. It is not uncommon that this happens. What is required of the neutral, by law as well as by ethics, is that he/she bracket feelings and remain impartial and objective in relation to all disputants. What helps in retaining neutrality is for the mediator always to focus on enforcing a fair process and successful communication among the parties.

A third crucial element to accent is that in mediation the disputants retain the power of decision-making; the decisions they make and the agreements they come to and sign off on are their own and not forced or imposed by a third party. This is perhaps the primary reason mediation appeals to disputants: they retain for themselves the power to make decisions affecting their lives and futures, instead of having decisions imposed by third parties. Accordingly, it is important for mediators to emphasize, when explaining mediation, that their role is not that of a judge or jury but that of a process facilitator. It is the parties in dispute who are empowered by the mediation process, not a third party, as in litigation and arbitration. Indeed, in mediation the disputants are encouraged not to agree to any outcomes that they do not like or that they believe are not beneficial to them. As in negotiation so also in mediation, those whose interests and needs are at stake are at the same time stakeholders who alone have the power to decide future outcomes.

Mediation is emerging in contemporary societies as a compelling and distinctive way of resolving certain kinds of disputes. It is finding an important niche in our court and legal system between negotiation, on the one hand, and litigation, on the other. Not only is it generally successful in resolving conflicts,[4] it is beneficial to the courts for two reasons, because it is a cheaper alternative to arbitration and litigation and it eases the court's backlog of cases.

VALUES AND PRINCIPLES

What values and principles underlie the mediation process and contribute to its capacity for resolving conflicts? What qualities endow mediation with its power to facilitate cooperation and agreement among even hostile parties? At least five qualities pertain to its success.

First, mediation attempts to discover *root causes* of conflict specific to the case. The tendency of parties in dispute is to argue issues and neglect causal conditions that generate them. But conflicts are not likely to be resolved nor relationships transformed unless underlying causes are understood and addressed; unless disputants are encouraged to look below the surface clash and treat substantive causes and needs from which conflicts arise. Fear and anger often accompany and intensify conflicts; understanding the conditions that foster these emotions is crucial to finding common and enduring resolutions.

Secondly, mediation guarantees a *fair and just process* without which resolving conflict satisfactorily is quite impossible. Most conflicts arise in relationships characterized by power imbalances. In most disputes, one party typically possesses more power than the other party, whether that power is in terms of resources, knowledge, status, expertise, and so on. Mediation establishes a context in which power imbalances are neutralized; each party makes decisions in the context of a fair process and equal decision-making power. It is not uncommon for disputants in mediation to find themselves listening fully for the first time to the concerns and needs of the other (often less powerful) disputants. Guaranteeing equal power goes a long way toward putting parties in position for resolving disputes. Equal power is a precondition of agreeable solutions.

Thirdly, according to principles of mediation, substantive conflicts between disputing parties presuppose substantive *common ground;* that is, the needs and interests treated and addressed by mediation are fundamentally compatible, not incompatible. One of the benefits of a neutral third party is the "distance" the neutral maintains in relation to the conflict and disputants, so that she can see commonalities that the disputing parties are not in a position, at least initially, to see. One of the benefits of the stages to the mediation process is that they lead disputants in a direction from which they too can begin to see commonalities that not only accent conflicts but constitute a basis for communication and agreement. The neutral, then, helps the disputants explore their common needs and interests as a way of arriving at creative and satisfactory solutions.

Fourth, the possibility of resolving conflicts involves a *restructuring* of the relationship between disputants. This restructuring is guaranteed by the mediation process itself. It undermines the inequalities characteristic of hierarchical relationships and places parties on equal footing, at least for the duration of the mediation itself and for the sake of agreement. Not only in the process does this restructuring take place, but also in the outcome. In litigation and arbitration, power to dictate outcome is surrendered to a third party, so that the imbalance of power amongst disputants themselves is never addressed. In mediation both parties not only retain equal procedural power but retain equal executive power; so that ideally not only in mediation but also in their ongoing relationship a restructuring takes place that facilitates future communication and resolution.

Finally, mediation requires an enhanced understanding and practice of *communication skills* in a way that other models of dispute resolution do not. Because the neutral is not an advocate for either party and because power of agreement lies with disputants, it is incumbent on them and on the mediator to employ skills that effectively communicate and promote agreement. Our discussion in later chapters will include skills that help parties communicate instead of alienate, that open up instead of close down cooperation, skills that require the speaker, instead of the other, to bear responsibility for what is said. Since the burden of resolving conflict lies with the disputants and not a third party, they mutually benefit themselves by actively listening and collaborating with the other. This skill of active listening is not always easy to cultivate but it is essential both to the success of the mediation process and to a successful, ongoing relationship between the parties.

You will soon learn the stages of the mediation process. These stages are not just convenient markers to persuade parties toward agreement; they are calculated to foster a psycho-social peacebuilding dynamic; one that enhances self-understanding and a reciprocal, mutual understanding of each other, so that both arrive at a place where even hostile parties can find common ground for peacemaking and agreement.

This dynamic, peacebuilding process entails deepening dimensions of intra- and interpersonal engagement and understanding (see figure 2.2):

(1) The most fundamental dynamic of mediation's process is self-examination and self-understanding. Sometimes persons in conflict do not fully know what their OWN interests and needs and desires are until they are given a fair chance in front of the other to articulate and discuss them. Especially during the Story-Telling and Clarification Stages each disputant is encouraged to articulate how they view the cause of the conflict and what their basic needs and interests are in the conflict. (2) Secondly, mediation's

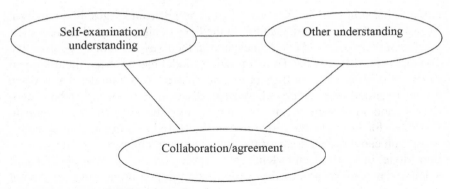

Figure 2.2. Peacebuilding Dynamic

peacebuilding dynamic promotes between disputants a clearer and fuller understanding of the needs, interests, and desires of the other. Very often mediation is the first time the disputants have been "forced" to listen to each other more fully than they have in the past. Indeed, sometimes the conflict perpetuates itself because each has not listened carefully to the other, each has not understood the interests and needs of the other. Mediation provides a safe and fair space in which each disputant can be confident of being heard and understood, perhaps for the first time. Especially when a neutral summarizes and feeds back the story of each party, a reciprocal dynamic of self- and other-understanding takes place. (3) Finally, this ongoing reciprocal dynamic, this process in which each party comes to understand herself and the other more clearly and fully, situates each in relation to the other in such a way that they are able to come to an awareness of common ground, after which a collaborative, formal agreement on most if not all issues is possible. Most mediators experience a "magic" moment when disputants turn and begin to talk to each other in a civil and constructive way. That is the moment in which the hard work of communication and process yields a harvest of creative, constructive resolutions. Accordingly, not only does negotiation and problem-solving occur but very often also a foundation is laid for ongoing peaceful relations; for a degree of interpersonal transformation that enables disputants to trust each other, continue a relationship, and successfully communicate.

TRANSFORMATIVE CONFLICT RESOLUTION

The values and principles of the Transformation Model are ancient and enduring. They can be found in the cultural practices of indigenous peoples and tribal customs; in the message of great prophets and sages, like Lao Tzu, Moses, Buddha, Jesus, and Gandhi; in the lives of simple and obscure societies, like monasteries and communes; and in the lives of ordinary people, like you and me. Although the Transformation Model has not been the dominant model of dealing with conflict throughout history, it is a model that is often highly regarded and celebrated. We can discover its values in labor negotiations and in current social movements, like the civil rights movement. Consider, for example, the modern civil rights tradition in the United States. See if you can discover some of the values and principles of the Transformation Model in Martin Luther King Jr.'s classic *Letter from Birmingham Jail,* a letter that can be accessed at www.thekingcenter.org/archive/document/letter-birminghm-city-jail-0.

In 1963 Dr. King was arrested and jailed for leading a protest march. While in jail he received a letter from a group of Alabama clergymen objecting to his presence in Birmingham; accusing him of being an "outsider" and of unnecessarily stirring up trouble and promoting violence. Dr. King's *Letter* is a reply to these clergymen. He advocates a precarious path of Transformation between the Domination and the Prevention Models, between violence and complacency. Dr. King's "campaign for non-violent civil disobedience" negotiated a path of compromise that impacted an entire nation and transformed the way diverse, even hostile, disputants interact with each other. Complete Exercise 4 below to trace the similarity of transformative principles and values manifest in mediation and Dr. King's campaign.

INQUIRY AND REFLECTION EXERCISES

1. Earlier you described a conflict you were recently in. Continue your analysis by explaining what you believe to be the root causes of the conflict, any power imbalances between disputants, and any communication skills that you or the other person used.

2. Describe a personal experience in which you found yourself, perhaps unexpectedly, playing the role of a third-party neutral, helping two friends or family members settle a dispute. Then, assess how you did in that facilitator role. Did you help them find common ground and solve the dispute? Why or why not? Did you feel comfortable in your role as a third-party neutral?

3. Access the Internet and find an article regarding labor negotiations or an article regarding an arbitration case. Briefly describe the process and the outcomes.

4. Access and read Dr. King's *Letter from Birmingham Jail* at www.thekingcenter.org/archive/document/letter-birmingham-city-jail-0. Identify and explain parallels you see between mediation's Transformation Model of peacemaking, its values and principles, and the values and principles of King's campaign for nonviolent, civil disobedience.

NOTES

1. Barbara A. Nagel Lechman, *Conflict and Resolution,* Second Edition (New York: Wolters Kluwer, Aspen Publishers, Second Edition, 2008), 13.

2. William D. Kinsey, et al., *Mediator Communication Competencies: Problem Solving and Transformative Practices* (Boston, MA: Pearson Custom Pub., 5th ed., 2005).

3. Samuel Forlenza, "Mediation and Psychotherapy: Parallel Processes" in *Community Mediation: A Handbook for Practitioners and Researchers,* eds. Karen Duffy, James Grosch, Paul Olczak (New York, NY: The Guilford Press, 1991), 228.

4. Barbara Nagel Lechman states that "studies indicate that a mediated agreement is more likely to be complied with than a judgment imposed by a judge." See *Conflict and Resolution*, Second Edition (New York: Wolters Kluwer, Aspen Publishers, 2008), 65.

3

Sources and Styles of Conflict

SOURCES OF CONFLICT

Conflict is one of the more prevalent and persistent features of human experience, whether in the form of internal tensions or interpersonal disagreements, whether in the form of community discord or national disputes, whether of political posturing or civil war, of regional struggle or global. Not surprisingly there are available to societies and cultures a variety of "styles" for dealing with conflict, some more successful than others, some favored by a culture and others not. But in all cases, understanding the origin and nature of conflicts and various "styles" for dealing with them is crucial to resolving them. This chapter takes small steps toward examining a variety of sources of conflict, the power dynamics of these sources, and various styles for managing them.

Think of a conflict you currently face. Think of international conflicts your nation is currently engaged in. Often people occupy themselves with trying to resolve conflicts without examining the origins and root causes of them; they simply compete while often neglecting to search out sources. Think of two conflicts—Afghanistan 2002–present and Iraq 2003–2011—engaged in recently by the United States, which were responses to the terror attacks of 9/11. To what extent did the public and its leaders engage in a substantive process of discovery, of examining the causes of the acts of terrorism? Not surprisingly, discovering the sources of conflicts is critical to understanding and developing a strategy for resolving them. What are the major and perennial sources of conflicts?

A wide variety of schemes have developed for sorting through and categorizing sources of conflict, categories that apply equally to interpersonal and

Table 3.1.   Sources of Conflict

Resource Sources	Needs Sources	Values Sources
Economic	Survival	Beliefs
Property/energy	Power/authority	Morals/rights
Time	Communication	Cultural style
Knowledge/skills/ technology	Privacy/identity	Priorities/principles

international tensions. Three general categories are often identified, under each of which fall more specific sources (see table 3.1).

The origin and root causes of most conflicts can be situated somewhere on this scale of categories, recognizing that most conflicts are generated by multiple causes.

Access, acquisition, and availability of *resources* are major sources of conflicts at all social and personal levels. Restrictions placed on resources and their uneven distribution domestically, nationally, and globally generate seemingly intractable tensions and disputes. Family members struggle for access to and acquisition of resources; social and economic and ethnic classes struggle for access to and control of local resources. Consider for example the tensions between Florida and Georgia over access to water; or international spats over extracting and developing resources; drilling for oil, for example, or fracking; native access to salmon and fishing rights, access to and distribution of limited medical technology and organs for transplant.

Secondly, individuals and societies are often driven by *basic needs* that are considered essential for survival and comfort. Some needs are common to all, such as food and shelter; other needs vary, such as the kind of transportation available. Needs, it is true, sometimes are functions of expectations more than necessities; nevertheless, what is an expected need for transportation in New York City is not the same as what is the expected need in rural Nebraska or Africa. Sometimes resolving conflicts requires the painful process of examining human needs/expectations and the extent to which they may be sources of and grounds for resolving it.

Finally, consider conflicts that arise from beliefs and moral *values*; for example, disputes over abortion—right to life versus right to choose, evolution or creation, immigration reform, global warming, economic equality, minimum wage, gun control or not, responses to terrorism, how to raise and educate children, and so on. Conflicts over these important matters often emerge from people holding steadfastly to principled beliefs and values. Such convictions are the foundation and framework for managing life with civility; but they are also the catalyst for much seemingly intractable conflict.

So, neutrals need to have always with them questions like: What are the sources of these conflicts? How does knowing about sources help people manage and resolve conflicts?

CONFLICT AND POWER DYNAMICS

Power imbalances sometimes intensify conflicts. It is important for neutrals to understand the manifold ways in which these imbalances manifest themselves during mediation. *Power is the extent to which a person is able to exert control over and influence another.* To try to get the other party under one's control is a familiar dynamic of human relationships and usually expresses itself during mediation sessions. Most conflict includes some measure of power imbalance and as a result involves a measure of fear, mistrust, and anger. Accordingly, no doubt "Issues of anger, mistrust, and fear are best dealt with by confronting the feelings, discussing the feelings";[1] but ultimately even these feelings must be dealt with by confronting the power imbalance in the relationship. The mediation session does just that, at least for its duration; it provides a fair and safe context for neutralizing the imbalances and adverse feelings they generate. During the mediation session power imbalances take various forms and are expressed in diverse ways. I discuss six common ways, all of which overlap and interact one with the others. All of them are employed by disputants as leverage to threaten and intimidate, to manipulate and try to get what they want.

First, one of the most common ways power is asserted is in terms of *resources*. One party in the dispute asserts an advantage over adversaries by possessing or managing greater resources of one sort or another. The resource may be in the form of money or property or other material goods; or may involve power of greater access or control of such resources. Think of ways resources are ordinarily used for advantage. A spouse might say, for example, "I'm not going to continue paying for your outrageous credit card bills if you don't agree to get rid of the card"; or the government may say to a petroleum corporation, "To approve access to drilling on federal land in the Arctic your company must show that it has the capacity both to prevent damage to the environment and the ability to rehabilitate it if a spill occurs." Resources are often a source of power and power imbalance.

Another use of power by one party over another involves *expertise*. Some try to gain advantage and control over others by virtue of some special knowledge or skill that the other party does not have or have access to. "I've been in real estate for years. I know what's best for financing our house. You can decide how to landscape and decorate it, but leave the financing to me";

or "I'm a nutritionist; Robert doesn't even know how to feed himself in a healthy way; I don't trust him to be able to feed our daughter nutritious food when she visits him." Of course, we all have expertise and skills that others do not. It is important to draw on these benefits; but to use one's expertise as a tool to leverage advantage over another is abuse of that power.

People sometimes use who they know and *associate* with to their advantage and as leverage to get what they want. "Networking" is a normal part of personal and professional life, but to use associations as a way of controlling or manipulating colleagues to get one's way misuses power. An employer's kin or a professor's students are given preference and promotions even though they may not possess credentials and experience equal to other applicants. In local government, association sometimes leads to abuse, such as a builder who provides gifts and benefits to an official in exchange for certain public contracts. Associations, of course, are important in professional life and should be cultivated. But to exploit them for one's advantage unfairly over others is to undermine the integrity of those relationships.

Legal power and the threat to appeal to it is a ploy commonly used in disputes and in mediation sessions. It is wielded as a kind of sword of Damocles to leverage consent to one party's desires. It takes various forms: threat to sue; threat to take the issue to court if one party does not get his way (e.g., promotion, sole custody). Very often, in court mandated mediation sessions, a court order and date is already established; sometimes that order is used by parties as a threat to secure a more favorable agreement. Appeal to the law and the courts are a power that is attractive to many disputants. The risk of taking a case to court, however, is that decision-making power no longer resides with the disputants but now with a third party.

Power and influence is sometimes unavoidably based on *position* and status. A person's relative status in an organization automatically confers on that person a certain legitimate authority over others. Humans live with this power dynamic daily: a boss, a president, a vice-president, a dean, a CEO or CFO, a professor, senior partner, parent, and so on. Position confers a certain status to which belongs legitimate power, albeit power limited by professional regulations and protocol and ethics. From the corner convenience store to Wall Street, from employee to employer, from city manager to president, from student to teacher, from child to parent, power dynamics institutionalize themselves in terms of position and status. Those with power of position are easily tempted to exploit that power to their own benefit while imposing undue burdens on those of lesser status.

Sometimes power is simply *coercive;* a person informally "takes things into his own hands" and randomly grants power to himself absent any appeal to other authority. Coercive power revolves around a personality that attempts through fear and intimidation to control, impose, bully, and dominate others. Usually through some form of demagoguery, through manipulation, this person tries to impose on others his views, his decision. "If I don't get my way I will take our daughter and leave the state." Instead of appealing to law and legitimate authority, coercive personalities are willing to undertake extraordinary actions that sometimes transgress laws or violate protocol.

Other forms of power precipitate inequalities and contribute to conflict. Ordinary life is saturated with power imbalances; we all live every day in relation to them: parents and children, teacher and students, boss and employees, civil authority and citizens, laws and daily life. It is not the imbalances themselves that are problematic and cause conflict; we expect and accept them. Rather, it is the misuse and abuse of them: the angry, overbearing father or boss, the overly aggressive police officer, or an intrusive interpretation of laws. All official formats for resolving conflicts—negotiation, mediation, arbitration, and litigation—arrange themselves in ways calculated to counter and neutralize abuse of power. One advantage of mediation is the specific way it is able to counteract and nullify such abuses, by enlisting five techniques. These techniques together contribute to the equal empowerment of parties in conflict. In the next three chapters we will see how they are structured into the mediation session.

Mediation guarantees first of all a *fair process*. This means that all parties will be given equal opportunities—to hear and be heard, to discuss and ask questions, to communicate and brainstorm. Part of the problem in many conflicts is the fact that one or more of the voices have been habitually silenced or ignored. Sometimes for the first time in mediation parties hear and listen to each other. Secondly, mediation guarantees *fair access*. To a certain extent information is power and equal access to information is important in finding common and level ground on the basis of which to work toward agreement. Whether full disclosure of financial information in labor negotiations or in marriage and custody arrangements, equal access to relevant information is important to resolving disputes. Thirdly, mediation guarantees *fair enforcement* of rules and regulations. Not only do neutrals guide the mediation through the steps of a fair process, they also enforce equally with all parties certain rules of effective communication. All are equally subject to the same rules; for example, refraining from interruptions and *ad hominum* attacks, active listening, using certain communication skills like "I" statements, and so on. Fourthly, mediation guarantees to each party *equal decision-making power*. The neutral has no power to decide what is best for resolving issues in a dispute; the parties in dispute alone retain equal power to agree or not agree to a particular proposed resolution. This is part of the great appeal of mediation in contrast to litigation and arbitration; substantive decisions are the prerogative of the disputants themselves. And finally, mediation guarantees *fair outcomes*. One responsibility of a neutral is to make sure that all points of an agreement are fair and just; that is, that all points of agreement meet the needs and interests of both parties equally, including the interests of constituents (like children) to the dispute. Sometimes a party feels pressure from the other to agree to something that may not be in her best interest; a neutral is responsible for bringing this to the attention of the party, perhaps by caucusing. So, although not making decisions regarding the substance of an agreement, a neutral does protect each party from signing an agreement that may not entirely be in her interests.

These mediation techniques for neutralizing power inequalities have proven effective in placing even hostile disputants in a position to come to fair agreement on important and substantive issues. In subsequent chapters we will learn just how it is that the mediation process and the neutral are able to accomplish this goal of equal empowerment, of nullifying the power imbalances that precipitate conflict. This balance is partly accomplished when neutrals understand the various styles by which humans manage conflicts.

STYLES OF MANAGING CONFLICT

Along with peacemaking models (Domination, Prevention, Transformation), personal conflict styles provide patterns whereby individuals, communities, and societies interact with and respond to conflict. Patterns develop into habits and often become so deeply rutted in the psyche that identifying and altering them requires extraordinary self-examination and effort. Understanding the nature of these styles is important for mediators if they are to assist disputants in surmounting fears and expectations that prevent progress toward common ground and agreement. Typically, five styles are identified. Most people practice all styles at one time or another, but usually develop habits that favor one or two. All styles are under certain conditions appropriate and under certain conditions inappropriate. What is your favored style(s) of managing conflict? What are the origins (e.g., parental model, etc.) of your habits in responding to conflict? How aware are you of shifting from one style to another in attempting to resolve conflicts?

Avoiding

Avoiding seeks to steer a person clear of conflict. The ways that a person eludes conflict may be physical or psycho-social; people may withdraw physically from contexts in which they otherwise would face conflict; or they may intentionally ignore or bracket conflict when it arises. Reasons for doing so vary, of course: fear of the result of conflict on a relationship, anticipation of discomfort, power imbalance, and so on. In limited circumstances, avoiding may be appropriate; for example, when one has little power in a relationship and the issue is not deemed that important. But generally habitual avoidance is not terribly healthy for relationships, for families, friends, or businesses. Harmful feelings and even bitterness will likely emerge and undermine the relationship. Hence, if a relationship is ongoing and relatively important, then avoiding is inappropriate and often harmful.

Accommodating

This style seeks to sustain a relationship by obliging the other person and adapting to his desires and needs. If this style is used habitually, for the sake of gaining acceptance or deferring important issues, resentment often follows. Appropriate reasons for doing so may include a desire to sustain a relationship when the issue is not so important as to risk damaging or ending it. Generally, accommodating as a persisting habit is healthy only insofar as it is reciprocal, only insofar as each party is willing at times to accommodate the interests of the other. Spouses, for example, may alternate selecting TV shows to watch, what music to listen to, or what restaurant to dine at. But if accommodating is habitually one-sided or if the issue is significant to both parties, then the pattern of accommodating may be destructive and undermine respect.

Competing

By competing, persons directly confront issues and each other in order to gain a goal or secure benefits that are important to them. Suspect reasons for competing may include feelings of insecurity or of superiority or a desire to "win at all costs" or to "teach a lesson" to the other: for example, gang conflict or hostile corporate buy-outs. Competing as a habitual style often damages and injures irreparably relationships that otherwise may be important to maintain. Reasons for confronting, however, may be constructive, if an issue is morally significant or highly valued: for example, when parents deem "tough love" important for the welfare of children or when human rights inspire people to acts of civil disobedience in order to draw attention to injustices and to persuade or even non-violently coerce authorities to negotiate fair resolutions. Sometimes when repeated habits of avoidance and competing combine they form a habit of passive/aggressive behavior that is generally damaging to relationships if not entirely destructive.

Compromising

Compromising is a style in which all parties are mutually willing to concede certain benefits and/or accept certain burdens in order to achieve a conciliatory settlement. This familiar style commonly requires a reciprocal "give and take" on the part of all parties. Sometimes motivation for compromising is sheer exhaustion from conflict that is intense and intractable. Political stalemates over budgets, for example, often "get resolved" in this way, often with regrets from politicians on both sides. Compromising, however, can be constructive and rewarding; especially when parties see the benefits and burdens as more or less equally distributed and ultimately to their advantage. Children as well as adults have a keen sense of fairness and often perceive such reciprocal arrangements as desirable and satisfactory. International mediation and diplomatic negotiation, such as the 1978 Camp David Accords, often entail compromises that are perceived as roughly reciprocal and preferable to sustained conflict.

Collaborating

As a step beyond compromising, collaboration presupposes a significant degree of mutual respect and a confidence in the reliability of the mediation process and neutral, if not in the reliability of the other party. This style involves substantial levels of cooperation: people working as partners toward solutions that are ultimately satisfactory for all, a win/win. Since collaboration requires significant time and energy and attention it may not be a style appropriate to issues that are minor or pressing. Yet, collaboration is the preferred style when the relationship is important and enduring and when the issues and outcomes are significant to success and to sustaining a relationship. Resolutions to conflicts that arise in marriages, in businesses, or in social movements like civil rights, appropriately employ collaboration for achieving outcomes that are significant to the welfare of many. Divorcing parents who realize the benefit to their children of joint legal and residential custody exemplify collaboration at its best.

It is important that neutrals understand the dynamics of conflict represented by these five styles. The ability to manage conflict during mediation sessions and direct it toward creative and constructive outcomes requires a neutral skilled in recognizing conflict styles and how they are used during mediation. Very often, all conflict styles manifest themselves during a single mediation; they can be forces either for good or ill, depending on the skill of the neutral to direct and redirect them toward constructive ends.

CONFLICT, DIVERSITY, AND BIAS

Racial, ethnic, gender, developmental diversity, and cross-cultural training is, of course, essential to the success of mediation and to resolving conflict. Some refer to "diversity competence" as a skill neutrals should master; a skill whereby a neutral (a) empowers disputants of different races, ethnicities, cultures, genders/sexual orientations, disabilities, traditions, and experiences to freely express themselves; and (b) facilitates a process wherein disputants are encouraged to craft agreements based on their own distinct priorities, perspectives, and values. Not only is doing so in mediation required ethically, but legally as well. Mediation functions within the legal context of several federal laws:

Title VII of the Civil Rights Act of 1964: prohibits discrimination based on race, color, religion, sex, and national origin.

Title IX of the Education Amendment of 1972: requires education programs to assume responsibility for preventing and ending sexual harassment and violence.

Americans with Disabilities Act of 1990: prohibits discrimination against people with disabilities.

In addition, mediation centers should be prepared to provide upon request an interpreter/translator when language is a barrier to communication, as well as be prepared to provide equal access to technology.

Diversity and cross-cultural competency requires mediation and neutrals not only to accommodate diversity but to encourage and promote it. Doing so requires a delicate balance between providing an environment and process that is entirely impartial for all disputants, on the one hand, and that encourages the expression of difference—racial, ethnic, cultural, developmental, religious, and gender identity difference—on the other. Indeed, mediation establishes a framework that sustains both poles of this balance, by affirming both impartiality and difference. How so? First of all, mediation provides impartiality by guaranteeing:

- a neutral meeting site and environment,
- a neutral third party mediator, and
- a neutral process and procedure.

By guaranteeing these, disputants in all their differences can be confident of fair and equal treatment as well as fair and equal outcomes. Within this impartial framework, secondly, mediation and neutrals encourage each disputant to find and express his/her own voice and empowers them to search for agreement outcomes based on unique individual identities, values, priorities, and needs.

Furthermore, if mediation and dispute resolution are to be successful, neutrals must be entirely self-aware and self-vetting in regards to their own biases and prejudices. All people, including neutrals, have preferences, biases, and prejudices, which, if unattended or neglected, might very well undermine a climate of diversity and impact negatively the fairness and success of dispute resolution. What is the neutral to do? First, be fully honest and aware of one's own biases and prejudices, and what their causal conditions are; secondly, know fully what their triggers are, and how and when they may contribute to conflict; thirdly, in the context of the mediation session, learn how to bracket preferences and prejudices so they do not interfere or endanger the success of the neutral's impartiality and the fairness of the session. For example, a neutral might have a personal bias against people who wear visible tattoos, because years ago as a child he was frightened by a gang of bikers whose tattoos became a symbol and trigger of that fear. Being self-aware of this experience and its source assists the mediator in neutralizing the impact of that fear and bracketing the bias against the disputant with tattoos. Or a neutral, raised in a conservative family, might have a moral and social bias against the lifestyle of transgender people. What must this neutral do to counteract the negative impact of his bias against a transgender disputant?

INQUIRY AND REFLECTION EXERCISES

1. Identify and briefly discuss (a) one personal example each for the three kinds of "sources" (resources, needs, values) that caused conflict in your own experience; (b) one national or international example each for the same three kinds of "sources."

2. Continue your analysis of the conflict you described earlier. Examine it in terms of the conflict style(s) you used to deal with the conflict. Did you use one style and then another? To what extent were you successful in resolving the dispute using one of the styles?

3. Draw a pie circle calculating each conflict style you use as a slice or percentage of the whole. Be ready to give examples of each style.

4. Online, investigate the dispute between Georgia and Florida over access to water; or investigate the dispute between the Lummi native tribe in Washington State and its struggle to obtain and maintain fishing rights. What are the sources of the conflict? What action has been taken to resolve the conflict?

5. In his *Letter from a Birmingham Jail* Dr. King discusses his program for securing civil rights; in doing so he explains how he favors one style of managing conflict over other styles that he rejects. Explain how he places his own style of managing civil rights' conflicts (collaborating) in the context of these other styles: avoiding/black complacency and competing/black nationalists.

6. Make a list of your most significant biases and prejudices. Then, explain in writing for each bias (1) the origin and root cause of that bias, and (2) what you might do as a neutral to control and neutralize its impact on your ability to conduct a mediation session fairly.

7. Complete the Conflict Management Styles Quiz; source is Reginald Adkins:

WHAT IS YOUR STYLE OF HANDLING CONFLICT?[2]

Rate each statement on a scale of 1 to 4 indicating how likely you are to use this strategy.

1 = Rarely, 2 = Sometimes, 3 = Often, 4 = Always

- Answer questions how you would behave rather than how you think you should behave.

1. I explore issues with others so as to find solutions that meet everyone's needs_____
2. I try to negotiate and adopt a give-and-take approach to problem situations_____
3. I try to meet the expectations of others_____

4. I would argue my case and insist on the merits of my point of view_____

5. When there is a disagreement, I gather as much information as I can and keep the lines of communication open_____

6. When I find myself in an argument, I usually say very little and try to leave as soon as possible_____

7. I try to see conflicts from both sides. What do I need? What does the other person need? What are the issues involved?_____

8. I prefer to compromise when solving problems and just move on_____

9. I find conflicts challenging and exhilarating; I enjoy the battle of wits that usually follows_____

10. Being at odds with other people makes me feel uncomfortable and anxious_____

11. I try to accommodate the wishes of my friends and family_____

12. I can figure out what needs to be done and I am usually right_____

13. To break deadlocks, I would meet people halfway_____

14. I may not get what I want but it's a small price to pay for keeping the peace_____

15. I avoid hard feelings by keeping my disagreements with others to myself_____

HOW TO SCORE THE CONFLICT MANAGEMENT QUIZ

As stated, the fifteen statements correspond to the five conflict resolution styles. To find your most preferred style, total the points in the respective categories. The one with the highest score indicates your most commonly used strategy. The one with the lowest score indicates your least preferred strategy. However, if you are a leader who must deal with conflict on a regular basis, you may find your style to be a blend of styles.

STYLE CORRESPONDING STATEMENTS: TOTAL

Collaborating: 1, 5, 7 _____
Competing: 4, 9, 12 _____

Avoiding: 6, 10, 15 _____
Harmonizing: 3, 11, 14 _____
Compromising: 2, 8, 13 _____

BRIEF DESCRIPTIONS OF THE FIVE CONFLICT MANAGEMENT STYLES

Collaborating Style: Problems are solved in ways in which an optimum result is provided for all involved. Both sides get what they want and negative feelings are minimized.

Pros: Creates mutual trust; maintains positive relationships; builds commitments.
Cons: Time consuming; energy consuming.

Competing Style: Authoritarian approach.

Pros: Goal oriented; quick.
Cons: May breed hostility.

Avoiding Style: The non-confrontational approach.

Pros: Does not escalate conflict; postpones difficulty.
Cons: Unaddressed problems; unresolved problems.

Harmonizing Style: Giving in to maintain relationships.

Pros: Minimizes injury when we are outmatched; relationships are maintained.
Cons: Breeds resentment; exploits the weak.

Compromising Style: The middle ground approach.

Pros: Useful in complex issues without simple solutions; all parties are equal in power.
Cons: No one is ever really satisfied; less than optimal solutions get implemented.

NOTES

1. Lechman, *Conflict and Resolution*, 29.
2. The source of this quiz is "The Conflict Management Style Quiz," by Reginald Adkins, at Elementaltruths.com.

II

PROCESS

4

Preparing for Mediation

ORIENTATION: REFERRALS

Neutrals and mediation centers receive cases to mediate from a wide variety of sources, formal and informal. Formal sources include the courts, social services, social workers, police departments, juvenile detention centers, attorneys, law offices, clergy, churches, school officials, teachers, and so on. An especially important source for referrals is the courts. Parties can be referred to mediation by the courts in at least two ways: (1) as soon as two or more parties formally file a complaint with the court, the Clerk's office can direct that case to mediation while the parties wait for a court date/appearance; or (2) a case can be mandated to mediation by a judge, when she sees that the case might very well be resolved privately by the disputants instead of publicly by the court. Police and social workers may refer parties to mediation when disputes arise between parties and no criminal activity is involved. Informal referral sources are becoming increasingly common. Awareness of mediation as a viable format for conflict resolution is spreading, as is access to trained neutrals. Most communities in North America have direct access to mediation services, whether provided by the courts or by private organizations or by professionals. Furthermore, mediation's reputation as an effective, less costly, and highly successful means of conflict resolution is gradually growing and becoming general knowledge. Individuals and corporations increasingly choose to retain neutrals instead of lawyers to mediate certain kinds of conflicts.

ORIENTATION: INFORMATION EXCHANGE

Prior to a formal mediation session, it is usual for the parties to independently exchange information with a neutral or intake assistant. This exchange of information may take place in person at a mediation center or via a phone call or email, although security and confidentiality is a constant concern. Two kinds of information is typically exchanged: intake and introduction to mediation.

(1) Intake information from disputants orients the neutral not only to the nature of the dispute, but to some of the specific issues that may arise, for which background research might be appropriate. Typically intake information will include the names and contact information of the disputants; any constituents (personal or corporate) related to the dispute, who may be affected by an agreement; whether the case is mandated by the court, including the court date, and so on. In addition, ordinarily separate paragraphs are written down, one for each of the parties in dispute. Each paragraph provides a brief description of the conflict from the perspective of each party. These paragraphs provide the neutral with a brief introduction to the issues of the dispute; such information may assist the neutral in several ways: for example, indicate that research by the mediator before the mediation session may be helpful; indicate that the neutral may need to request that the disputants bring with them certain information and documents. Some neutrals, however, prefer to begin mediation as a *tabula rosa*, with an entirely blank sheet, without any knowledge of the facts and issues involved in the case. In this way they can mediate spontaneously, without preconceived notions about the parties and thereby minimize any personal preferences or prejudices.

An **Intake Form** might look something like the one shown in figure 4.1.

(2) Disputants involved in mediation should also prepare ahead of time for the mediation session. The most basic preparation is information. Before the first mediation session, the neutral (or intake assistant) will inform each party of the nature and process of mediation and what they can expect in and from the mediation session. The neutral, in other words, briefly explains what mediation is, its purposes and procedures. Preliminary information also includes the nature of confidentiality and exceptions to it, fees, the fact that signed agreements are legal documents, the date and time of the mediation session, any documents that the parties should bring with them, and answers to questions the parties may have.

PREPARING TIME AND SPACE

Time and space are important to successful mediations. There is no magical, instantaneous resolution to mediated conflict; it takes time and energy and

INTAKE INFORMATION FORM

Date of Mediation_____

Case Number: Mediators Name:

PARTY ONE

Party One: Phone Number:

Email: Address:

Constituents:

Brief Description:

PARTY TWO

Party Two: Phone Number:

Email: Address:

Constituents:

Brief Description:

Figure 4.1. Intake Information Form

intentional deliberation. No authority pronounces or declares a decision; the disputants themselves work through a procedure that puts them in a position to come to agreement regarding their respective desires and needs. An intentional procedure is undertaken: the stages of deliberation and the time they take are usually well worth it; well over three-fourths of mediated cases are successful. Typically, a single mediation session lasts for about two hours; if further time is needed additional sessions are arranged until a full and satisfactory agreement is concluded. In the next chapters I will discuss each stage of the mediation session itself and certain communication skills that make success possible.

Courtrooms are arranged in an orderly way conducive to its distinctive procedures: the judge as authoritative figure positioned prominently, with other players—lawyers, defendants, juries—situated "below" in relation to that authority. Likewise, mediation lends itself to a particular orderly arrangement of space conducive to its own character. That arrangement should include:

- *Neutral space.* Mediation sessions should be held in a neutral space, not in a space that one party identifies with and the other does not. Feeling disadvantaged by territory does not cultivate the trust and respect needed for mediation. Mediation centers typically provide neutral space. At places of employment conference rooms are often sufficient. If the mediation session is conducted as shuttle diplomacy or as extended caucusing, then comparable rooms and facilities should be provided for all parties.
- Since decision-making power is equally distributed amongst disputants and since the neutral retains procedural power, physical space and *arrangement of furniture* should reflect that distribution. If the disputants agree to mediate within the same space (i.e., the same room) then the furniture (table, chairs, etc.) usually are arranged so that the neutral(s) are situated equidistance from the parties in dispute. It is important to avoid any appearance of favoritism or partiality, even in terms of space and time. Traditions and preferences vary on how to best situate disputants in relationship to each other. Some neutrals prefer that disputants sit across the table from each other, so as to be a safe distance from each other and so as to make eye contact, with the neutral(s) seated equidistant in-between. If disputants are seated next to each other, it is thought, each might feel that their personal space and safety are compromised. Other neutrals prefer that disputants sit next to each other, facing the neutral, and not across a table facing each other. Much is communicated non-verbally and facially. If disputants sit facing one another, it is thought, it is likely that the adversarial and antagonistic relationship will intensify. If they sit next to each other facing the neutral, communication is more likely to take place between them through the auspices of the neutral. Furthermore, the chairs for each disputant should be the same, the same size and style. Any appearance of difference may give one party the sense of being disadvantaged by the other's "power seat."
- Equal access to *communication technology.* Disputants may want the opportunity, during the mediation session, to contact lawyers or constituents via phone or email or texting. A private space for these activities should be equally available to disputants.
- *Flip charts or smart boards.* Especially during the problem-solving stage it is important to have available a medium to write on. For example, it is

often helpful for the neutral to make lists of interests, one for each party; each list should note the interests/issues each would like to see resolved. It is helpful for all parties to visualize the list of interests they are to discuss and resolve.

ACTIVE LISTENING AND CONFLICT GRID

The most fundamental and fundamentally important communication skill in mediation, as well as in life, is "active listening." Active, effective listening is a skill all parties—both neutrals and disputants—need to cultivate. It is the skill by which the neutral focuses on and listens for specific details in what a disputant is saying; it is the skill that will help the disputants construct solutions to issues and eventually a signed agreement. Often while listening, people are distracted in a variety of ways—by prejudices, by expectations, by one's own thoughts, by preparing a reply, while the other is speaking. Or if not distracted, people often fail to listen with purpose; they hear but don't listen for selected and important details. A neutral needs to learn the skill of actively listening for certain specifics that will be helpful in facilitating an agreement between the parties. Particularly, the neutral will listen for the details of what is called a "Conflict Grid." These details include issues, hot buttons, interests, relevant facts, BATNAs (see page 45), and possible solutions. Students learning the skill of mediation and active listening usually benefit from sorting through and sorting out the material by using a grid, such as represented by the form shown in figure 4.2.

Actively listening with purpose is clearly a neutral's most important skill; all of the details of a Conflict Grid are crucial for finally putting the parties in a position where they can, with the help of a neutral, make a satisfactory agreement regarding the issues and interests that matter to them.

Disputants. The Conflict Grid first asks the neutral to identify *the parties/disputants* directly involved in the conflict. How many "sides" are there to the conflict and who are the parties directly involved in it? For purposes of simplicity, this book follows the model of a two-party conflict; but very often conflicts involve more than two. For example, cases of sexual harassment in the workplace involve the accuser, the accused, the employer, and other employees. Along with identifying the parties directly involved in the conflict, the neutral should listen for and identify *constituents* to the parties in conflict. These are people or groups who, although not directly involved in the conflict, have interests in the outcome or are likely to be impacted by the outcome. In the case of workplace harassment, for instance, the EEOC (Equal Employment Opportunity Commission) is a constituent; it has an interest

Mediation Conflict Grid

Mediator Name:_____   Date:_____

Party One:_____   Party Two::_____

Constituents:_____   Constituents:_____

	Disputant 1	Disputant 2
Issues (Hot buttons)		
Interests		
Facts		
BATNAs		

Possible Solutions: 1, 2, 3, etc.

Figure 4.2.   Mediation Conflict Grid

in protecting civil rights in the workplace and might have a representative present at mediation. In child custody cases children and grandparents are clearly constituents who are impacted by mediated decisions. Neutrals should ask about possible constituents whose interests are at stake or who may be impacted by an agreement.

Issues. Neutrals actively listen for *issues*; these are the material, behavioral, and tangible concerns that disputants articulate; they are *what* can and must be resolved; the measurable outcomes the disputants want to achieve through mediation. Issues constitute the *what*, the tangible, material matters that are actually in dispute and can be successfully mediated. Issues are concerns expressed by disputants that lend themselves to discussion and successful, negotiated resolution. Issues are some of what needs to be addressed for all disputants to consider the mediation session successful; collecting unpaid bills or rent, for example, or agreeing to a visitation schedule for a non-custodial parent. The neutral helps the parties distinguish these issues from (1) personal *feelings* and attitudes, and from (2) personal *positions* advocated, both of which are important but not matters that are mediated and resolved.

First, emotions and *feelings* are often prominent in disputes and in mediation sessions. Mediation should provide a safe framework in which even intense feelings can be expressed; they should not be ignored or marginalized; rather they should be acknowledged as "hot buttons" and important to the disputant and to understanding the character of the dispute. Yet the primary business of mediation is not to heal ill feelings and interpersonal hostilities, although that may result. A mediated resolution, for example, may not alter the disgust one party feels toward the other's irritating habit of complaining about report deadlines; but a deadline for reports and submitting late reports are issues that can be civilly discussed and resolved. In short, many factors contribute to the tension and intensity of the conflict in a mediation session, but not all of them can be negotiated, especially interpersonal feelings and attitudes, prejudices and animosities. These more subjective dimensions of conflict are important but beyond the purview of mediation and mediators. They may require therapy not provided by mediation. Neutrals are not therapists and should not attempt therapy. It is true that during mediation sessions a great deal of healthy (or unhealthy) emotional "venting" may occur; that is fine and inevitable. But neutrals are equipped to be facilitators not therapists; they need to actively focus on issues and interests common to the relationship of the parties. In child custody cases, for example, very often the divorcing parents feel intensely hostile toward each other and may both feel that the other is inadequate as a parent. These feelings are often expressed but cannot be mediated; indeed they may be feelings mutually felt even though and when all the issues related to child custody have been successfully resolved.

In actively listening for issues, however, the neutral at the same time is actively listening for "hot buttons." Hot buttons are those issues to which each party has the strongest emotional reaction, the issues about which each party demonstrates the most passion and concern. The mediator can indicate in the Conflict Grid each "hot button" by placing that particular issue in parentheses (   ). Indeed, we shall see that in mediation, strong feelings associated with certain hot button issues should not be ignored or rejected but accepted and acknowledged. But ultimately the focus of mediation is on issues and concerns that are interactive between the parties and are susceptible to collaborative agreement, even though strong feelings may remain. The victim of sexual harassment in the workplace may retain the fear and hostility toward a coworker even though an agreement is worked out in which the perpetrator no longer is allowed to interact professionally with the victim.

Secondly, *positions* are intractable stances taken by each party, based on personal opinions and biases that are generally in opposition to and exclusive of the stance taken by other disputants. School teachers may take the position that standardized testing and teaching to standardized tests is intrusive, unnecessary, and a waste of time and resources. Those same teachers, without relinquishing their stance, may nevertheless work with administrators/advocates of standardized testing: sorting out a reasonable schedule for mandated testing and implementing best practices for educating children. It is incumbent on neutrals, then, to develop the skill of distinguishing *issues* from *positions*. Positions are generally intractable, non-negotiable stances that alienate disputants from each other and which are not susceptible to negotiated resolution; they are personal convictions that parties take that barricade them off from one another. Issues, on the other hand, are objective concerns all parties to a dispute have in common; these concerns are what brings disputants to mediation in the first place and are what hopefully bring them together through negotiated agreement.

Interests. Interests are closely linked to issues, as their personal source and motivation. Issues are the objective outcomes, the *what* a disputant wants to accomplish through negotiation; interests are a person's subjective motives, the *why* a disputant desires to negotiate a particular issue and outcome. A simple example: a worker wants to negotiate a more favorable benefits package (issue) because she is getting married and planning to have children and desires financial security (interest) for her family; or, a teacher insists that students arrive to class on time (issue) because timeliness exhibits respect (interest) for teacher and other students, whereas tardiness exhibits disrespect. In general, issues are measurable, tangible matters that are negotiable between disputants; interests are intangible, personal desires, needs, and expectations held separately by a disputant; they are intangibles that motivate a person to engage in mediation and work toward negotiating a particular issue; satisfying the interests of disputants is important to getting agreement on specific issues.

An essential skill neutrals must cultivate, then, is the ability to distinguish between issues and interests; between objective matters that can be mediated, and subjective motives and needs. But although interests are not negotiable, they constitute an underlying condition that should not be ignored; as the sources that generate negotiable issues, interests must be acknowledged and addressed by the neutral if a disputant's needs are to be satisfied and a negotiated settlement secured. Indeed, many neutrals insist on an "interest-based" strategy for conducting mediation sessions; a strategy in which neutrals first focus on eliciting dialogue regarding personal interests, needs, and motives as gateways to identifying issues that are accordingly susceptible to mediated agreement. If genuine transformation is to take place through mediation, it is thought, then neutrals must assist disputants not only in problem-solving common issues, but also in addressing and satisfying personal interests and needs.

Facts. The neutral also must listen actively for *facts* that bear directly or indirectly on the conflict and its resolution. These facts are not issues or interests *per se,* but they do have some relevance and significance for understanding the nature of the conflict and possibilities for agreement. Some of these facts are related to the dispute's history: When did disputants begin to notice disagreements? How and why did conflict first arise? What caused disagreement originally? What are its sources? How has the disagreement changed over the months/years? What are the key events shaping the conflict in its current form? The parties may disagree in answering these questions, of course; but the business of the neutral is NOT to sort through them to get to the truth. Rather the neutral's business is to listen for these important facts and see how they may contribute to understanding the history of difficulties and to resolving them. Other facts are important, such as whether there are any written documents or evaluation of performance; whether there is a court order; whether any attempts, formal or informal, have been made to resolve the dispute. Every case has its own array of facts that should be noted. The neutral is responsible for actively listening for and retrieving them; they may contribute to agreement.

Some of the facts and information may very well be in dispute; parties may disagree regarding them or may disagree about their importance. Sometimes "what the truth is" regarding matters is not held in common by the parties. The business of the neutral is not to determine "who is telling the truth and who is not." Disagreements of this sort are usually symptoms of the dispute itself and sometimes important for one party in distinguishing himself from the other. Generally, however, parties agree about most important facts, even though interpretations may differ.

BATNA. Another item a mediator should listen for or ask about is referred to as a *BATNA.*[1] This acronym stands for *Best Alternative to a Negotiated Agreement.* It refers to the course of action each party independently plans to take if mediated negotiations fail and a satisfactory agreement is not achieved. BATNA is a kind of bottom line for each party, and mediators would do well to ask about it if it is not voluntarily expressed during the mediation session: "What course of action do you plan to take if an agreement is not reached today?" Common BATNAs include taking the matter to a higher authority, like a boss or supervisor, or settling it in a court of law. It is common for parties to think that if they take the matter to court the judge would likely rule in their favor. It is also not unusual for them to ask a neutral her opinion: whether a court is likely to rule in his/her favor if the case ends up in court. Of course, the neutral does not know and should not venture an answer. Other common BATNAs relate to the various sources of power parties believe each has over the other; these sources are sometimes used as power plays, as ways of threatening the other and of trying to leverage an agreement in his/her favor; for example, a threat to quit a team or job, submit a formal grievance, deny a promotion, or get someone fired. Some BATNAs, whether expressed or not, may be informal or even illegal, such as sabotaging a project or taking a child out of state (kidnapping). However, BATNAs can also be an occasion for the neutral to remind the parties of the advantage afforded them by pursuing a negotiated/mediated agreement: namely, that in mediation decision-making and signed agreement remain in their power; most resolution alternatives place decision-making power at the mercy of others or of circumstances.

Solutions. And of course neutrals actively listen for *possible solutions* that emerge intentionally or incidentally during a mediation session. Any agreement or any part of an agreement is properly "owned" by the disputants. A neutral, however, may need to inquire about possible solutions that he has heard during the course of the session. What constitutes a possible solution? A solution may consist of something as simple as a verbal apology and as complex as an institutional plan that requires time and energy to implement, like a five-year labor and benefits contract. In all cases, a solution consists of any action or behavior that addresses successfully for the disputants one or more of the issues and interests listed in the first two rows of the Conflict Grid. Indeed, possible solutions should parallel and address directly listed issues and interests. A full agreement provides solutions to all of the issues and interests listed by all parties. One dimension of active listening, then, is for the neutral to focus on suggestions parties may verbalize regarding steps that might be taken to solve one or more or all issues and interests.

More will be said about each quadrant of the Conflict Grid in discussing the various stages of mediation. And more will be said about communication skills, active listening, and the qualities and techniques a neutral must use and teach in order to successfully manage the process of conflict resolution.

In this chapter we addressed how disputants and neutrals prepare for mediation, how to prepare the space in which to conduct mediation sessions, and how neutrals prepare for active listening (Conflict Grid). These techniques and strategies aim at providing a safe and comfortable context for the hard work of mediating; they are essential to its success.

INQUIRY AND REFLECTION EXERCISES

1. Recall the personal conflict you summarized in chapter 2. Complete a Conflict Grid based on your understanding of that conflict.

2. Find an article about an international or national conflict. Analyze the conflict, actively listening for the items listed on the Conflict Grid. Fill out the Grid based on your reading of the article.

3. Access the web page of the Supreme Court of your home state. Find out what the requirements, training, and criteria are for getting certified as a neutral. Write a list of the requirements for general mediation certification and the requirements for specializing in one area of mediation (domestic/family; small business, etc.).

4. You are a neutral for a mediation session. (a) Read and "actively listen" to the mediation transcript (Dale and Mary) below. Then, based on that reading/transcript, complete a Conflict Grid. (b) What possible fair and balanced solutions do you see as possible? (c) Also, pose two questions you might want to ask each of the disputants, based on their discussion with the neutral.

CASE: BUSINESS DISPUTE

Dale and Mary quite unexpectedly found themselves in court and the court mandated that they first take their dispute to mediation, to see if they could settle it. The date of their court order is in a month's time: October 21 at 10:00 am. Mary is somewhat disappointed to go to mediation; she thought that for sure she would get everything she wants in court.

Mary and Dale are co-workers at a small company, *Chip 'N Dale*, which makes computer chips. Dale owns the company and has worked hard for seven years to make a go of it. Mary is one of thirty-five employees, but she is different in that she is a graduate student and her work at the company is an internship. She is a single mother of one child, Sasha, who is four years old.

Both Mary and Dale finally agree to mediation. They agree that Mary should tell her side of the story first. "Initially," she says, "I thought I was going to like working here and for Dale. Things seemed right. He seemed like a nice guy; turns out he is a jerk and a flirt. He tells off-color jokes and makes inappropriate comments about women. It's embarrassing. He makes me feel very uncomfortable; I hate to come to work, but I have to survive and get my degree. But that's not the worst of it. He is withholding some of my pay and he refuses to pay for my daughter's healthcare. That's why I filed my suit, to get what he owes me."

Dale was eager to tell his side of the story. He started by saying: "This is the last time I'm ever hiring an intern from that damn university; what a joke she is: unreliable and inconsiderate as hell. Not only is Mary frequently absent from work; when she does come in she's often late, which throws everybody's work off. Everything we do is inter-connected; and if one person falls short it screws up the whole production process. A few times she even brought her child to work, saying her mother was sick and could not care for her, or some other excuses. Her supervisor's evaluations, frankly, have been mixed. She does acceptable work when she's here and focused; but he says she's not always focused and sometimes he says, she's rude and disrespectful of some of her co-workers, especially men."

Mary interrupted: "My internship allows me to miss work for classes; that's why I've missed work some."

Dale responds, "I have your class schedule; you've missed much more work than your schedule allows for; you're cheatin' on work and using classes as your excuse; you're just unreliable. I expect more from my workers, even interns."

Mary, "I'm afraid that as a result of my law-suit I will get fired. Not only will that destroy me financially; it will set me back in trying to get my master's degree."

I (the neutral) asked: "So, Mary, what do you want out of this mediation session?"

Mary, "I want everything I asked the court for: back pay that Dale has not paid me; re-imbursement for Sasha's healthcare costs, which is $376.00; and stop flirting with me by telling off-color jokes. Otherwise, back to court."

Dale replied angrily: "and I'll counter sue you; not only will I write a letter of evaluation to your academic advisor, what's his face, that'll bring your degree program to an abrupt halt, that's for sure. No way I'm going to pay you for work you didn't do; if you can't get here on time you don't get paid. And the contract says the company will pay healthcare for you; it doesn't say anything about healthcare for family members."

NOTE

1. This acronym was identified by Roger Fisher and William Ury in their book *Getting to Yes* (New York: Penguin Books, 1981).

5

Managing the Mediation Process: I

BEGINNING THE PROCESS

The successful resolution of conflict depends on many things: the willingness of participants to cooperate, the competence of neutrals, practicing certain communication skills, and completing the stages of a mediation process. When these forces converge conflict resolution is highly likely. In this chapter, and the next, the focus is on stages of the process itself and the communication skills relevant to success. These stages and skills are pertinent whether the mediation is conducted collectively, with all parties in a common space, or separately, with the neutral shuttling between private rooms.

Each stage of the process includes certain specific steps. It is helpful for beginners to follow the discipline of each step in each stage. Once learned neutrals can and should improvise according to their preferences and the needs of the disputants. Communication skills related to conflict resolution apply throughout the stages of mediation. Given this fact, I introduce various skills at stages where they tend to be most prominent and relevant. Active listening, the most basic and pervasive skill, I have already discussed; it applies throughout all stages of the mediation process. Consider a brief overview of the Stages of Mediation, the steps within each stage, and the relevant communication skills (see tables 5.1 through 5.5).

For each stage of the mediation process I will discuss its (1) purpose, (2) steps, and (3) skills.

Table 5.1. Stage One: Opening Statement

Steps	Skills
1. Expectations of disputants 2. Legal conditions 3. Confidentiality 4. Ground rules 5. Fees	• Organization • Clear, non-jargonistic language • Non-verbal/eye contact

Table 5.2. Stage Two: Story Telling

Steps	Skills
1. Party one story telling 2. Party one summary 3. Party two story telling 4. Party two summary 5. Repeat sequence of one and two for as many disputants there are	• Active listening • Summarizing (feedback) • Self-disclosing statements • Reframing

Table 5.3. Stage Three: Clarification

Steps	Skills
1. Clarifying questions 2. Common ground 3. List(s) of issues/interests	• Clarifying questions • Active listening

Table 5.4. Stage Four: Negotiation

Steps	Skills
1. Prioritizing 2. Generate and examine possible solutions 3. Identify solutions for each issue/interest	• Brainstorming • Caucusing • Summarizing solutions

Table 5.5. Stage Five: Agreement

Steps	Skills
1. Review each point of the agreement 2. Review who, what, when, where, how, and why 3. Confirm wording of each point of the agreement 4. Recommend review by attorney before signing	• Summarizing • Clear, non-jargonistic language

OPENING STATEMENT

The *purpose* of the Opening Statement is twofold—to inform and to build respect and trust. First the neutral explains the nature and process of mediation to the disputants. Most people do not know much about mediation and do not know what to expect. In addition, if the case is court mandated then the disputants are required to listen only to the neutral's Opening Statement. If they do not sign an "Agreement to Mediate" form then the case returns to the court. Courts are motivated to mandate mediation for several reasons: the effectiveness of mediation in solving certain kinds of cases, the reduced cost to the court of mediating instead of litigating cases, and the decreased backlog of court cases. So, it is important that the neutral explain clearly and concisely the nature and purpose of mediation and what can be expected. Secondly, many disputants are leery and uncertain about the capacity of mediation to solve their conflicts; so it is important to create an environment of confidence and trust both in the expertise of the neutral and in the effectiveness of the mediation process itself.

There are a variety of ways for a neutral to explain the *steps* that make up the mediation process. The one offered here is standard, but each neutral will want to develop his/her own way of presenting and explaining. The Opening Statement typically includes most of the following information.

1. The neutral introduces her/himself and welcomes the participants to mediation. She should congratulate them for agreeing to participate in mediation and assure them of its effectiveness in addressing their concerns. Also the neutral should confirm with them the name by which each party wants to be called. Most are happy to be addressed informally by their given name; others may want to be referred to by their family name or by a title.

2. Explaining the nature of mediation should be clear and concise. The neutral can ask whether either party has participated in mediation before. Then explain it by articulating a definition of mediation; for example, the one set forth in chapter 2: mediation is a process by which a neutral third party facilitates a process in which parties in conflict are able to discuss concerns they have so that they might come up with their own solution to each of their concerns. There are at least four items for the neutral to briefly emphasize: (a) that mediation includes several steps that put the parties in a position to come to an agreement; assure them that these steps include ample and equal time for each of them to state their desires and needs; (b) that as a neutral you are impartial; that you are not a judge or jury and do not decide for them what they should do; that your role is to facilitate a process; (c) that the power to make decisions about their concerns remains always with them and not with the mediator or anyone else. It is important to emphasize this distinctive

dimension of mediation—it empowers them, and not a third party, to make decisions regarding their future; and that (d) caucusing is an option and forum for resolving conflict. To caucus means that the mediator meets privately with each party to discuss pertinent matters. A caucus can be requested by either party and by the neutral, and is confidential. Caucusing will be further discussed in the problem-solving stage.

3. At this point in the Opening Statement the neutral should hand each disputant a copy of the "Agreement to Mediate" form (see form on pages 59–61) for them to look over. After they have reviewed the form, the neutral will briefly highlight certain key aspects of the form. (a) Legal matters and implications must be highlighted by the neutral: especially that each party is encourage to consult with legal counsel before, during, and after the mediation process; that for court mandated cases, signed agreements are contractual, and like other court documents legally binding, with the power of the court to enforce them; that before signing any written agreement the parties are encouraged to take it to his/her attorney to review it, to make sure interests are protected. (b) The neutral must explain how the mediation session is confidential. Legal confidentiality means that the court or any other authority has no access to information, no access to anything done and said, during a mediation session. This also means that neutrals cannot be summoned to court to testify regarding matters discussed in a mediation session or contained in case files. Parties can also decide to maintain confidentiality in other ways and venues as well. The neutral must identify exceptions to confidentiality. In most states, exceptions include suspected child or elder abuse or neglect and threats to harm oneself or others. A submitted signed mediation agreement is of course not confidential; it is submitted to the court for review; and (c) finally the fee for each party should be included on the "Agreement to Mediate" form and should be brought to the attention of each party.

4. Ground rules are important to the success of mediation sessions and should be discussed and affirmed. Common rules include:

- Respect each other: this means to speak respectfully to and about each other and to refrain from interrupting a person when the other is speaking. At this point the neutral will hand each party a piece of paper and pen, so that they can jot down notes instead of interrupting while the other is speaking.
- Be honest and open about all matters related to the case.
- Note that the parties can ask for and take a break (rest room, smoke, reduce tension) at any time during the session, as can the neutral.
- Since mediation is voluntary, the parties or the neutral can terminate the mediation session at any point and for whatever reason.

The neutral concludes the Opening Statement by asking the parties if they have any questions about mediation and what to expect from the mediation process.

Using good *communication skills* during the Opening Statement is crucial both for conveying information and for cultivating trust and confidence. These skills include:

- Establishing a clear, understandable, and orderly way of presenting (in the Opening Statement) introductory material to the disputants is essential. There is quite a bit of opening information to relay in a short time. You should find a clear and comfortable order of presentation, so that the disputants are not confused by it but feel more comfortable both with the mediation process and with the neutral. In order to gain trust they need to be clear about what to expect from mediation and from you, the neutral. I have arranged the Opening Statement above in a particular way that makes sense; but it is not the only way. If you find an order and sequence that you feel comfortable with, then the parties will most likely feel comfortable as well.
- As a dimension of the legal and criminal justice system, mediation unfortunately lends itself to jargon and legalese that is often confusing to participants; such "shop talk" should be avoided at all cost. Successful communication requires knowledge of one's audience and a use of language that is familiar and accessible to that audience. Professionals easily slip into jargon that is accessible to them but not to those outside their profession. So, speaking in clear, available language both communicates to and respects one's audience.
- Non-verbal communication is a vital way humans relate to each other; much can and is "said" non-verbally. During the Opening Statement and during the Story-Telling Stages, it is important for the neutral to be especially aware of non-verbal ways disputants communicate with each other and with the neutral. Think of the many non-verbal ways we communicate: eyes, facial expressions, body language and gestures, posture, tone, and volume of voice. Much is communicated non-verbally that a person might not be willing and able to express verbally. Sometimes what is said verbally is affirmed non-verbally, but sometimes contradicted non-verbally. A party may say "I can agree to that," for example, but gesture or roll eyes in ways that cast that affirmation in doubt. In a sense, then, the neutral must actively "listen" with eyes as well as with ears; we must read a person's eyes and gestures to understand completely what they are trying to communicate. In addition, a neutral should be conscious of how and what he is communicating non-verbally: eye contact or not; gestures,

attentiveness, facial expressions, body posture, etc. Especially when one party is speaking, note the non-verbal ways the other party responds.

STORY-TELLING

During the Opening Statement Stage the neutral does most of the talking. Not surprisingly, during the Story-Telling Stage the disputants do most of it. Indeed, the explicit *purpose* of this stage is to provide a safe space and time for each one individually to express his/her concerns, desires, and needs and to express how they feel about those issues that bring them to mediation in the first place. The implicit *purpose* of story-telling is to provide a forum in which each disputant listens to the other without interruption, often for the first time. In this way, story-telling initiates the vital process of self-examination/ understanding and understanding the other, a process that puts the parties gradually, eventually in a position to discover common ground for agreement (see chapter 2). Typically, the opportunity to tell their stories and "be heard" by the other and by the neutral further cultivates trust and rapport at least in the mediation process and in the neutral, if not trust in the other party.

The procedural *steps* for this stage are simple and straightforward.

1. In order to accomplish the transition from Opening Statement to Story-Telling, the neutral explains that "story-telling" provides each person a chance to talk about his/her concerns, desires, and needs. Then the neutral asks the parties "Who would like to tell his/her story first?" Usually the parties readily agree on who will go first. But, if even this decision causes disagreement it is common for the neutral to indicate which of the parties first initiated contact and ask if that party might begin.

2. First one party and then the other in sequence is given the opportunity to "speak her mind" regarding concerns, needs, and feelings and what outcome from mediation they would like to see. The neutral reminds the parties not to interrupt while the other is speaking and that a pen and paper is available for each to jot down notes as a recall prompt. Each party is given the opportunity to explain "the situation" as they see it from their perspective. At the same time that one party is speaking the other is listening and trying to understand the other's perspective. What is crucial to the success of this step is not simply the "telling" of the stories, but active listening by the neutral.

3. Active listening by the neutral is for the purpose of *summarizing*. Summarizing depends on the neutral's ability to verbalize the essentials of each party's story. The neutral "feeds back" briefly and concisely the essence of each party's story immediately after each story is told. This activity of summarizing is key not only for self-understanding but for understanding the other party as

well. Indeed, sometimes it is helpful, during story-telling, to give each party an opportunity to "summarize" what the other has said. Earlier I indicated what it is that the neutral actively listens for and summarizes, namely, the items of the Conflict Grid. But to practice these skills well is crucial to the success of this stage, especially mutual understanding and trust and rapport.

4. Usually all parties are given at least a couple of opportunities to tell their stories and to respond to the other party's "telling." The neutral should allow ample and roughly equal opportunity and time for each to speak and respond to the other, asking if they have anything to add to their stories. After each "telling" the neutral summarizes to reaffirm not only what is said, but that each party is indeed being heard and each concern taken seriously.

Employing and enforcing *communication skills* during story-telling is essential if understanding and agreement are to be achieved.

- Active listening and summarizing are two interactive skills that the neutral must exercise during story-telling. See the discussion of active listening in chapter 3. What the neutral actively listens for is also what the neutral "summarizes" when feeding back the essentials of each story. Recall that active listening is focused and targeted; specific items are listened for, and these same items are what the neutral summarizes. And what is actively listened for, and hence summarized, is each category of the Conflict Grid: interests, hot button feelings, facts, and BATNAs, although not possible solutions. The neutral, after each story-telling, feeds back in summary form to each party the details of these categories of the Grid. Feelings and hot buttons should not be ignored or dismissed. Venting is a therapeutic part of the mediation process, even though mediation is not therapy and the neutral is not a therapist and should not pretend to be one. Emotions nevertheless are important. Even though they are not interests that can be mediated, it is important to acknowledge and affirm them.

Some neutrals prefer to allow disputants to tell their stories without interruption from the neutral, without the neutral interrupting with questions. Other neutrals prefer to ask pertinent questions during story-telling. My own preference is the former strategy, leaving questions for the Clarification Stage. In either case, disputants should be allowed to tell their stories fully; most likely in the past they have been regularly interrupted by the other and unable to fully tell their stories.

- Often during the Story-Telling Stage and indeed throughout the mediation process the neutral will need to explain and require the parties to use "self-disclosing" or "I statements." These are statements in which the speaker assumes personal responsibility for what he is saying; he is claiming responsibility and bearing the burden of what he is claiming about the other person. "I" statements are crucial especially when what is being said is accusatory, when what is said charges, blames, criticizes, complains, incriminates, or denounces the other party. Self-disclosing acknowledges that what is said discloses the speaker's feelings, sense, attitude, and perspective toward the other party and not necessarily how things actually are. These are such introductory phrases as "My feeling is that X . . ."; "I think that X . . ."; "My concern is that X . . ."; "I would prefer that X. . . . " The weight of the blame or complaint expressed is borne by the speaker when self-disclosing statements are used. Doing so goes a long way to diffusing hostile emotions and reactions and thereby makes listening and civil communication more likely to take place. Finally, self-disclosing is one of the most fundamental and practical communication skills a person can cultivate; to employ it as a daily habit reduces dramatically occasions in which conflict can arise and flourish.

• Reframing is another critically important communication skill that the neutral must employ throughout the mediation process, including during story-telling. Reframing is only one of many labels for this skill; other labels include paraphrasing, neutralizing, and laundering language. Reframing is a skill in which the neutral spontaneously re-words and re-phrases language that is hostile, offensive, or insulting to the other party. The purpose for doing so is quite obvious: in order to remove the offensive language so that the party that is trying to communicate can be heard and actually listened to and understood. Not infrequently, what is said by parties in conflict is said to insult, demean, offend, shame, and humiliate. These are strategies used in order to "get the upper hand" and punish an opponent; they are common ways that the frustrations of conflict and the feelings generated by them manifest themselves. Of course hostile language not only complicates and intensifies and further alienates parties, it also obscures and detracts from the substance of what the speaker is actually wanting and trying to communicate. A neutral must be poised at all times to intervene in the conversation and ask the offending party to use appropriate language and to do this by reframing in non-offensive language the underlying point the speaker is trying to communicate.

These first two stages (Opening Statement and Story-Telling) provide a foundation for successful mediation. A neutral who expertly guides disputants through them likely places the disputants in a position to come to an agreement that satisfies the interests and needs of both.

INQUIRY AND REFLECTION EXERCISES

1. On an 8 × 5 inch index card, develop a list of prompts for verbalizing your own comprehensive Opening Statement. Arrange them in a way that makes sense to you and then practice articulating your OS to another person.

2. From a distance observe two or more people talking; this may be in a cafeteria or café or library or park or city street. Describe the non-verbal ways in which they communicate with each other—from gestures and facial expressions to tone and volume of voice. Based solely on non-verbal expressions explain what you interpret them to be communicating to each other.

3. Complete the "I" Statements exercise sheet; see page 61–62.

4. Complete the Reframing exercise sheet; see page 62–63.

AGREEMENT TO MEDIATE

We the undersigned parties agree to voluntarily enter the mediation process and understand and consent to the following:

1. **Definition of Mediation**: Mediation is a process in which a mediator facilitates communication between the parties and, without deciding the issues or imposing a solution on the parties, enables them to understand and to reach a mutually agreeable resolution to their dispute.
2. **Role of the Mediator**: The mediator acts as a facilitator, not an advocate, judge, jury, counselor, or therapist. The mediator assists the parties in identifying issues, reducing obstacles to communication, maximizing the exploration of alternatives, and helping parties reach voluntary agreements.
3. **Mediator's Style/Approach**: *(for example)* The mediator uses a facilitative approach. A facilitative mediator guides the parties' conversation and discussion of issues that are important to them, without providing an opinion or judgement regarding the merit of the claims or the likely judicial outcome. The mediator can assist the parties in assessing the strengths and weaknesses of their case. The mediator will not tell the parties what to do or suggest a particular outcome.

4. **The Mediation Process**: The process will include at a minimum, an opportunity for all parties to be heard, the identification of issues to be resolved, the generation of alternatives for resolution, and if the parties so desire, the development of a Memorandum of Understanding or Agreement.

5. **Other procedures to be used during the mediation include**: *(for example)* caucus; the ability of any party or the mediator to terminate the mediation.

6. **Confidentiality**:

All memoranda, work products and other materials contained in the case files of a mediator or mediation program are confidential. Any communication made in or in connection with the mediation, which relates to the controversy being mediated, including screening, intake, and scheduling a mediation, whether made to the mediator, mediation program staff, to a party, or to any other person, is confidential. However, a written mediated agreement signed by the parties shall not be confidential, unless the parties otherwise agree in writing.

Confidential materials and communications are not subject to disclosure in discovery or in any judicial or administrative proceeding except:

   (i) where all parties to the mediation agree, in writing, to waive the confidentiality,

   (ii) in a subsequent action between the mediator or mediation program and a party to the mediation for damages arising out of the mediation,

   (iii) statements, memoranda, materials and other tangible evidence, otherwise subject to discovery, which were not prepared specifically for use in and actually used in the mediation,

   (iv) where a threat to inflict bodily injury is made,

   (v) where communications are intentionally used to plan, attempt to commit, or commit a crime or conceal an ongoing crime,

   (vi) where an ethics complaint is made against the mediator by a party to the mediation to the extent necessary for the complainant to prove misconduct and the mediator to defend against such complaint,

   (vii) where communications are sought or offered to prove or disprove a claim or complaint of misconduct or malpractice filed against a party's legal representative based on conduct occurring during a mediation,

   (viii) where communications are sought or offered to prove or disprove any of the grounds listed in § 8.01-581.26 in a proceeding to vacate a mediated agreement, or

   (ix) as provided by law or rule.

7. **Mandatory Reporting**: According to Virginia Code §63.2-1509, if mediators have reason to suspect that a child is abused or neglected, they must report the suspected abuse immediately. Therefore, the information about the abuse is not confidential.

8. **Complaints Against Mediators:** If someone who is not a party to the mediation files an ethics complaint against the mediator, confidentiality will be waived to the extent necessary for the complainant to prove misconduct and the mediator to defend against the complaint.

9. **Full Disclosure of Assets:** In domestic relations cases involving divorce, property, support or the welfare of a child, each party agrees to provide substantial full disclosure of all relevant property and financial information.

10. **Legal Counsel / Effect of Agreement:** The mediator(s) does not provide legal advice. Parties are encouraged to seek the advice of independent counsel at any time. Any mediated agreement may affect the legal rights of the parties. Each party to the mediation should have any draft agreement reviewed by independent counsel prior to signing the agreement.

11. **Fees:** (*if applicable*) The fee arrangement is as follows: _____

Plaintiff/Petitioner	Date
Plaintiff/Petitioner Attorney	Date
Respondent	Date
Respondent Attorney	Date
Mediator	Mediator

"I" STATEMENTS EXERCISE SHEET

The aim of "I" or self-disclosing statements requires the speaker to assume responsibility for what is said and claimed. They place the burden of what is said on the one speaking and not on the other about whom the speaker makes a claim. It is beneficial for the neutral to require "I" statements of disputants; it both diffuses defensive reactions to accusatory statements and it allows the message of what is being said to be more effectively heard and communicated.

Exercise Example:

1. Accusatory: "Dan, you're lying, and you know it."
2. Self-disclosing: "Well, Dan I certainly see things differently than you."

Revise the following as "I" statements.

Exercise One:

1. "You don't even feed yourself nutritious food. So, how are you going to be able to feed our daughter what she needs to be healthy?"
2. _____
   _____

Exercise Two:

1. "The project would have been completed on time if you had paid attention and done your part."
2. _____
   _____

Exercise Three:

1. "About half the time you're late to class. That's an insult to other students and to me. If this were a job you'd be fired."
2. _____
   _____

REFRAMING EXERCISE SHEET

The aim of reframing is for the neutral to re-state in a neutral and accessible way what a disputant has said in an insulting and alienating way. Often disputants communicate in angry, fearful, and hostile language. The duty of a neutral is to reframe or paraphrase what is said so that the hostility and offensive language is "laundered" and the core of what the disputant wants to say is effectively communicated. The reframing should be in neutral and positive language and might begin with phrases such as, "You value" or "You would like" or "What you prefer" or "What would be helpful to you" or "What I believe you are saying." The neutral must look beyond the hostility and negativity for the *underlying* sense of what the speaker is trying to communicate.

Exercise Example:

1. Offensive: "What a lazy slob. I could've finished that job in half the time. And you call yourself a professional."
2. Reframed: "What you would like is that everyone on your team complete projects in a timely and professional fashion."

Exercise One:

1. "You are irresponsible; you left the place a disaster so I had to clean your mess up before guests came."
2. _____
   _____

Exercise Two:

1. "You're a lyin' cheat. You estimated that repairs would cost about $1,500.00. $2,300.00 is not even close. Not a chance you'll steal that much from me."
2. _____
   _____

6

Managing the Mediation Process: II

CLARIFICATION

The *purpose* of the Clarification Stage of the mediation process is transitional; it both looks back to Story-Telling and forward to Negotiation. Based on what the neutral has heard in story-telling, this stage seeks both to identify and clarify interests and issues related to the categories of the Conflict Grid and to establish common ground; these matters need to be settled in order to proceed to problem-solving and negotiation.

1. The first *step* is for the neutral, who has been taking notes, to clarify matters regarding things said or inferred during story-telling. The neutral may have questions regarding the history of the dispute, regarding facts, personal interests, the current nature of the relationship between the parties, and so on. Sometimes one of the parties may be hesitant to say much during Story-Telling. Clarification Stage is an opportunity for the neutral to encourage that party to talk further about her concerns and what she needs and wants from mediation. Or the neutral might caucus with her (see pages 69–70) to discover if there are matters she is reluctant to talk about in front of the others.

2. The second *step* is for the neutral to highlight commonalities or common ground underlying the tensions and disagreements. This is especially important because the disputants, in telling their stories, are usually highlighting their differences and expressing hostilities. At this point it may very well seem to them that the same old issues that have plagued the relationship for some time are insurmountable and all hope of achieving agreement lost. So it is worthwhile to help the parties see that their differences are partly a result of common ground, of overlapping interests, concerns, needs, and hopes. To do this, it is important for the neutral to reassure the parties that despite dif-

ferences, agreement is indeed possible. An obvious generic commonality, of course, is that both parties have common ground just in coming to mediation, not only because they are experiencing in common a particular conflict but because they share a goal, namely, to resolve their common conflict. But the neutral can and should draw attention to more substantial commonalities. In family disputes, when children are constituents, for example, the neutral can note: "Although you have experienced a great deal of heartache, you are here because you want the best for your kids; I can see that for both of you the welfare of your children comes first. Because of that, I believe you will be able to make significant progress toward agreement." Or, in corporate conflict, the neutral might note: "You both seem to know that in order for the company to secure this major contract both of your teams will somehow have to find a way to work together; otherwise, as you both mentioned, many employees are likely to be laid off. I can tell that neither of you like that prospect." The threat of joint termination tends to get employee attention. Common ground becomes the basis for assuring parties of the possibility of progress toward agreement.

3. The final *step* is for the neutral to help parties identify and clarify the specific, concrete issues and interests that they would like to see resolved; issues expressed during story-telling. The neutral has been taking note of issues, interests, and possible solutions; but it is the parties, not the neutral, who identify and take ownership of what they want to resolve. Hence, the neutral asks each party to make their own list of issues; the neutral writes the lists of items on the available flip chart. All parties can then not only see that their concerns are taken seriously and will be addressed, but come to see and understand the priorities and concerns of the other party. Each item constituting the two lists (one list for each party is common) is identified by a word or a phrase; no need for complete sentences. The neutral should ask each party if his/her list as written is acceptable and complete, and assure them that they can add items later if they would like. Lists for a domestic dispute and child custody case might look something like:

Party A	Party B
1. Credit card expenses	1. Vacations
2. Child care-giver	2. Child's extracurricular activities
3. Visitation schedule	3. Visitation schedule
4. Child support	4. Nutrition for child

All *communication skills* discussed earlier are, of course, relevant during the Clarification Stage; especially active listening, summarizing, enforcing self-disclosing statements, and reframing. One additional communication skill is relevant, the technique of asking appropriate questions in order to elicit from the parties helpful information and to clarify interests and perspectives. Two kinds of questions are common—closed and open-ended.

- Closed questions elicit "yes" or "no" answers and are typically used to clarify or confirm facts or a party's perspective or expectations. For example: "You did say, didn't you, that you could alter your schedule to accomplish this project?" or, "The date of your up-coming court order is what?" Generally, the answers to closed questions are simple and straightforward.
- Open-ended questions attempt to generate further comments and perspectives on important topics and concerns and needs. Open-ended questions tend to ask who, what, where, when, why, or how, in order to generate more information and perspective. If one party is especially quiet and reluctant to offer views, the neutral should ask questions that draw him out: "Talk more about why you don't want your children to stay overnight at Dave's apartment?" Or, "How long do you think it will take you to finish this project and what kind of assistance will you need to complete it?"
- During any stage, including the Clarification Stage, the neutral might ask each disputant to feedback and summarize what the other is or has been saying. As already noted, getting them to listen to and understand each other is crucial for making progress toward agreement. Sometimes mediation is the first time they have had to try to understand the other.

NEGOTIATION

This crucial stage of the mediation process is perhaps the most difficult of all, because it asks disputants to cooperate, to find common ground that helps them discover collaborative solutions to their disagreements. Disputants do engage in "transformative problem-solving" at this stage, by which I mean a process in which the neutral facilitates a conversation between disputants that engages them at two levels—interests and issues. That is, the neutral finds ways to help disputants transform their relationship and share *interests* so that they can communicate directly, civilly, and successfully and on the basis of that transformation negotiate each *issue* successfully. The two—interests and issues—are inseparably connected, and should be treated that way. The demand for better work-benefits is intimately linked to the desire for increased financial security for one's family; the call for modifying standardized testing in the schools is a function of a desire by teachers for improving the quality of education. Accordingly, it is important for neutrals to guide the conversation beyond intractable, opposing positions (standardized tests constitute objective assessment criteria and are federally mandated versus quality education that engages the diversity of styles and interests of students ignored by standardized testing) to the common interest of both parties/positions, namely, to provide quality education for all students. The skill of neutrals to guide the discussion from intractable positions to common interests is essential to finally finding a solution to specific issues (how often to give standardized tests; how to accommodate diversity and encourage different learning styles and outcomes) and satisfying the needs of both parties.

To do so, the *purpose and aim* of the neutral now is to get disputants to brainstorm and bargain, to help them generate for themselves creative options that both satisfy their personal needs and interests and at the same time provide concrete solutions to specific issues (issues listed on the flip chart). Understanding interests and finding common ground is crucial, as noted earlier, to discovering solutions to issues, solutions that are generated and "owned" by the disputants themselves and not imposed by neutrals. Disputants always retain the decision-making power to agree or not to any particular solution. This power is one of the great responsibilities and appeals of mediation as a forum for resolving conflict.

1. The *steps* to negotiating interests and resolving issues begin with prioritizing; the neutral helps the parties decide which of the listed interests they want to begin with. There are good reasons to begin with a shared issue, or an easily resolved issue, or an urgent or most important issue. But however they begin, it should be the parties who decide. The neutral can ask each party to pick the issue they would like to begin with, and take turns selecting.

2. Secondly, for each issue discussed the neutral needs to be in control of the process/conversation. Disputants sometimes tend to wander from one issue on the list to another, and in doing so fail to linger long enough on any single issue to get it resolved. The neutral's challenge, then, is to keep the parties focused on one issue at a time. Of course, any one issue may incorporate other issues; but active listening on the part of each disputant and targeted discussion is critical to progress. So, (a) the neutral begins and guides the problem-solving process by asking each disputant to think about the first issue, and then to propose a solution to it that works for him/her. This reveals how far apart or near each party's proposal is to the proposal of the other. The neutral must keep in mind that in resolving issues disputants want their underlying personal interests satisfied as well. The neutral (b) then helps the parties negotiate in a collaborative and civil way, with the aim of moving progressively closer to a common, mutually acceptable solution to a specific issue. The skills and tools a neutral employs during negotiations include brainstorming, facilitating, and caucusing, which are discussed below. When

it appears (c) to the neutral that the parties have arrived at a shared solution to a specific issue, the neutral writes it down so that later on it can be reviewed and affirmed. Finally (d), this process is repeated until each issue/interest is addressed. The hope and expectation is that parties will come to a shared solution for each issue listed. The reality is that sometimes they will not be able to agree on a solution for every issue; these residual issues may have to be resolved through alternative formats. A large majority of issues, however, are resolved in mediation and the neutral should congratulate the parties on any and all successes.

Certain *communication skills* and techniques are vital to successful prob-lem-solving, especially skills of brainstorming, facilitating, and caucusing.

- Brainstorming is a strategy that aims at generating options and possible solutions to the list of issues established by the disputants. These options are the result of thinking imaginatively and constructively, guided by the neutral. Any decision to transform an option into a solution is solely the prerogative and power of the parties and not the neutral. However, brainstorming includes the skill of a neutral to ask questions that probe and prod the parties to think creatively and resourcefully about possible solutions, perhaps in new ways, in ways previously unimagined by them. Not only does the neutral ask open-ended questions, but she motivates the parties to ask imaginative questions of themselves and each other, in order to try to think in new ways about options and possible solutions. If the neutral sees possible solutions that the parties do not see, she must either get them to see them through questioning or ask permission of the parties to suggest them for consideration.
- The ability of the neutral to help the parties negotiate in good faith is sometimes daunting. Disputants are in the habit of disagreeing and defending positions instead of cooperating and endorsing each other. Facilitating a constructive conversation is pivotal: getting parties to con-sider and evaluate pros and cons of possible solutions; getting them to try and negotiate and perhaps blend proposals, granting a little to the other in order to get a little, is a common scenario for the sake of agreement. The neutral may ask them to consider options hypothetically: "What if you considered X as a possible solution. Do you see any possibilities for it resolving this particular issue?" Or "If you agree to X then what will the outcome be . . ., etc."
- Most neutrals find caucusing indispensable to getting to agreement. It is a private consultation between the neutral and each party separately, in a private room. The neutral should assure each party that a caucus is confidential; nothing said privately in caucus will be discussed publicly

in the mediation session, unless the disputant agrees to discuss it or permits the neutral to bring it to the table for discussion. Either the neutral or the parties can ask for a caucus. Caucuses should be relatively short and equal in length for all parties. There are many reasons and benefits for calling a caucus: to gather information from each party that otherwise they may be reluctant to discuss openly in front of each other; to address imbalance of power or threats; to alleviate and vent intense emotions; to identify BATNAs; to confer with a co-mediator; to break an impasse on a particular issue or concern. It is not unusual for disputants to reach an impasse on one or two listed issues. Instead of giving up on them, the neutral should ask for a caucus; it is often an effective way to make progress toward creative solutions on difficult issues. A disputant may be willing in caucus to suggest a possible solution that he is reluctant to present in the presence of the other party. The neutral should ask each party to be candid while reassuring them of confidentiality.

There are generally two sides to an impasse: discovering reasons for them and finding ways to overcome them. (1) Common reasons for impasse include one party's indifference to the issue; that the issue has not been sufficiently examined and understood; stubbornness; punishing the other; hidden agendas that present obstacles; and a determination to take a particular issue to court believing the court will resolve the issue favorably. (2) A neutral's techniques for overcoming an impasse include exploring root causes; discussing intense, hostile emotions, hot buttons, past injuries, and mistrusts that may prevent progress; exploring alternative solutions to those on the table; suggesting new compromises; pointing out unrealistic expectations; affirming progress that has been made on this and other issues; and reminding parties of consequences for failing to resolve an issue. The neutral might remind the parties of reality: that if they do not resolve the issues in mediation they may find themselves in court where their power to decide for themselves is surrendered to a third party.

AGREEMENT

This final stage of the mediation process is the material culmination of the hard work in the preceding stages. Its *purpose* is to write an official and formal agreement that is fair and balanced and meets the needs of all parties. A well-crafted agreement must meet at least two substantive criteria: (1) the issues and interests of the disputants and (2) the expectations of justice, each party treated with fairness and equity. That is why before signing it each party is encouraged to take any written agreement to counsel for advice.

Neutrals, accordingly, need to learn the mechanics of how to write a clear and concise agreement. The mechanics include the following *steps*:

1. Before writing the final draft of an agreement, the neutral should review with the disputants one by one each point of the agreement, making sure that the substance of each is agreeable to each party and that each point is stated in language agreeable to the parties.

2. In writing the agreement, begin with a general introductory sentence that states what the parties generally intend to accomplish by signing the agreement: "For the benefit and welfare of their children, Sara and Isaac, Mary and Joseph agree to the following settlement" (see an example on page 76).

3. Each point of the agreement (each resolution to an issue) should clearly specify WHO is agreeing to do WHAT, WHERE, WHEN, HOW, and perhaps WHY, insofar as each is relevant to that issue. Each point of the agreement should indicate certain specific behaviors that the parties will undertake in order to fulfill their obligations. Ambiguous words should not be used; words like "soon" or "friendly" or "keep the noise down" or "cooperate" are variously interpreted by people and do not specify what kind of concrete behaviors or actions would meet the expectations of one or both parties. How "soon" (date and time) is soon? What kind of behavior counts as "friendly" in the context of the relationship between the parties? In short, each point of the agreement needs to specify a concrete action/behavior that is expected and enforceable.

4. The neutral should encourage the parties to state each point of the agreement in language that is positive, realistic, clear, orderly, and balanced. If the agreement is long and involved the neutral should organize it into separate points (and sub-points if necessary) so that each point and behavior is easily understood and followed. Each point should use simple, clear language and avoid jargon; and each point should specify a more or less equal number of things that each party is responsible to accomplish. Moreover, the neutral should make sure that what is required of the parties is realistic, that the behaviors specified are actions that are within the power of the parties to accomplish.

5. Most official agreements will conclude with a final point in which the disputants agree to return to mediation if further conflict arises. The neutral should suggest this as a way of affirming what parties have already accomplished and as a way of encouraging communication and collaborative problem-solving in the future.

6. A standard, final paragraph to any written agreement asserts two things: that the parties are encouraged to take any written agreement to an attorney for review before signing it; and that a signed agreement is a legal document enforceable like any other court document.

Agreement writing, as a culmination of the mediation process, draws directly on most of the *communication skills* already discussed.

- The neutral must continue to listen actively, not only for possible solutions but now for clear and concise ways of articulating them and the behaviors that embody them.
- The neutral must then be able to summarize accurately each point of the agreement in order to get the endorsement of all parties. After reviewing each point, the neutral should ask if there are any other interests that the parties would like to discuss and resolve.

These are the mechanics of problem-solving and agreement writing. But much more than this is accomplished by skillful neutrals. Usually mediation sessions are occasions for peacebuilding, and for engaging more transformative matters, such as affirming personal interests, mutual respect, and trust amongst disputants; learning successful communications skills; and learning how to independently prevent future conflicts or transform them into creative, collaborative projects. This is the hope and promise of mediation.

A "Memorandum of Agreement" form will look something like the example shown in figure 6.1.

LAW AND ETHICS

Trained neutrals are educated in mediation law and ethics; they are familiar with general laws and moral principles and with those specific to a particular area of mediation, like family or business mediation. In this section I address laws and moral principles that apply to mediation in general. Those interested can access an elaboration of most of these principles online in an important document, *Model Standards of Conduct for Mediators* (2005), developed and published jointly by the American Bar Association, the Association for Conflict Resolution, and the American Arbitration Association.[1] Standards and laws vary to a certain extent from state to state; certified neutrals are trained in the laws and policies of the state in which they operate. A state's Supreme Court typically supervises and certifies neutrals and the training of neutrals. The following standards are fairly common. Many of them have already been set forth in the context of examining the mediation process.

Memorandum of Agreement
Valley Mediation Center
113 Madison St., Peaceville, MI
(900) 123-4567+Fax: (900) 765-4321+Email: VMCenter@Mediate.org

Date:_____

Mediator(s):_____   _____

Parties: _____   _____

Constituents:_____   _____

[Introductory statement]:

1.   Stated points of agreement

2.

3.

4.

5.

The parties are encouraged to consult with legal counsel before signing this agreement. If either sign without consulting counsel, the signature represents the voluntary waiver of the right to that consultation. By law, a signed mediation agreement is enforceable in the same manner as any other legal contract.

Signatures of Parties:

_____   _____

Figure 6.1.   Memorandum of Agreement

1. **Self-determination:** Self-determination is a distinctive principle of mediation that highlights its appeal and power. Mediation empowers the parties in dispute: (a) it promotes and protects "voluntary, un-coerced, decision-making in which each party makes free and informed choices" about the substance of any agreement and at any stage of the process about whether to continue; (b) it prohibits neutrals from forcing or influencing any party to enter into agreement.

2. **Impartiality:** The neutral will conduct mediation in a fair and impartial way. This means that she will not (a) favor any party in conducting the process, and (b) not show bias or prejudice toward the interests of one party or the other. One implication is that neutrals "neither give nor accept a gift, favor, loan or other items of value" that may compromise impartiality. The neutral shall inform all parties that the neutral does not provide legal counsel and is not an advocate for any party. If a party participates *pro se* (represents themselves in mediation without legal counsel) the neutral should inform them that they are eligible to have counsel present at any time during the mediation session.

3. **Confidentiality:** By law and ethics mediation is confidential. Legally this means that a court does not and should not have access to any information, subjects, viewpoints and behaviors occurring during the mediation session. The neutral shall treat as classified all mediation proceedings. There are, however, exceptions, including child and elder abuse or threat of harm to oneself and others; when all parties voluntarily waive the restriction of confidentiality; and the submitted, written, signed agreement itself, which is submitted to the court for review. Information from caucuses is also confidential, unless a party agrees to waive it.

4. **Competence:** Neutrals are expected to be properly trained, qualified, and certified to conduct mediation sessions "to satisfy the reasonable expectations of the parties." This means that they will be expert not only in conducting the mediation process but also expert in the particular area of concern and conflict, and that they will maintain their competence through continuing education.

5. **Diversity Competence:** Legally and morally neutrals are expected to be sensitive to matters related to disputant diversity. Neutrals are to

remain impartial and maintain impartiality among disputants regarding issues such as race, gender, sex, ethnicity, culture, and disability.

6. **Civil Immunity**: Neutrals and mediation organizations are immune from civil liability. This means that for any act or omission during mediation, the neutral is not liable to litigation, unless he/she has acted in bad faith or without regard to the rights and welfare of the disputants. Most states establish guidelines for determining neutral **misconduct,** which often includes (a) partiality, (b) providing legal advice, or (c) failing to inform disputants:

   • that a signed agreement has the legal status of a court document,
   • that prior to signing, each party can consult with independent legal counsel at any time, and
   • that each party is, may, and should have any draft agreement reviewed by independent counsel.

7. **Voluntary:** Mediation is voluntary for all disputants and for the neutral. This means that at any point during the mediation process any of the parties or the neutral can terminate the session. Neutrals have an obligation to consider termination when there is evidence or threats of abuse or violence or other criminal activity among the parties; or if the neutral determines that either or both parties are acting in bad faith.

8. **Fees and Costs:** As early as possible, the parties in dispute should be informed of fees and all other expenses of the mediation process. It is inappropriate and unethical for a neutral or program to establish contingency costs, a fee based on outcomes; and neutrals and programs are encouraged to provide some mediation at pro-rated or pro-bono rates.

9. **Marketing:** Neutrals and mediation centers are obligated to be truthful and honest in advertising their services, fees, experience, and qualifications. They should not guarantee outcomes or advertise in a manner that favors a certain kind of participant or in any other way that compromises the integrity of the neutral or mediation process.

These accepted standards are common sense for the most part. A neutral should become familiar with the ethics and legal code of the state in which they operate.

Memorandum of Agreement
Valley Mediation Center
113 Opie St., Peaceville, SH
(900) 123-4567+Fax: (900) 765-4321+Email: VMCenter@Mediate.org
Date: March 22, 2017

Mediator(s): Tallis Composario _____

Parties: Tina   **David**

Constituents: _____   _____

In order to resolve issues of communication, visitation, and child support Tina and David agree to the following:

1. Tina and David agree to go to family counseling to enhance their communication and parenting skills. Tina's current counselor (by April 3, 2017) will recommend a counselor for them.
2. David and Tina agree that Adrian will remain temporarily with his current childcare giver, Ruth Standberg, until David can interview her and approve her or not. If David does not approve of Ruth, both Tina and David will each identify a childcare giver to interview and approve or not.
3. Tina and David agree that Tina will have physical custody of Adrian. They also agree to joint legal custody. When David moves into his new residence, they will reassess custody arrangements.
4. David and Tina agree that every Tuesday and Thursday David will pick Adrian up at the childcare givers house at 5 and return Adrian to Tina by 8. Every other weekend, David will pick up Adrian from Tina Friday afternoon and return him to Tina's Sunday afternoon.
5. David will give Tina ample notice, via cell, if he would like to see Adrian at additional times.
6. Tina and David agree that every other Friday David will pay Tina $195 in child support for Adrian.
7. David and Tina agree that they can jointly work out holiday and birthday schedules for Adrian, when the time comes.
8. Tina and David agree that if additional issues and concerns arise or if they want to reassess the current agreement, they will return to mediation.

The parties are encouraged to consult with legal counsel before signing this agreement. If either sign without consulting counsel, the signature represents the voluntary waiver of the right to that consultation. By law, a signed mediation agreement is enforceable in the same manner as any other legal contract.

Signatures of Parties:

_____   _____

Figure 6.2.   Example Case Agreement

INQUIRY AND REFLECTION EXERCISES

1. Based on the transcript of the case of Dale and Mary (see pages 47–48), what (a) common ground can you as a neutral identify and articulate? (b) What two lists of issues would you write down (on a flip chart) for each? (c) What are the chief personal interests underlying Dale's issues and Mary's issues?

2. Explain whether you think that, as the neutral in the Dale and Mary case, caucusing would be beneficial or not. Give reasons for your answer. Explain why you would or why you would not caucus.

3. Analyze and evaluate the case agreement on page 76. For each point of the agreement discuss its strengths and weaknesses.

4. What should a neutral do?
   An employer calls a neutral and asks whether two of his employees have completed mediation. He also wants to know if they discussed and came to an agreement on a work-related project. He says that if he does not know by the end of the day he will have to terminate both of them.

5. Review the mediation code of ethics in your state of origin. Access the Supreme Court home page and click on the appropriate entry. Are there any principles that should be added to the list of principles in this chapter?

NOTE

1. All quotes following are from this document.

III

PRACTICE

Family and Domestic Mediation

FAMILY MATTERS

Family and domestic conflicts are often mediated; the courts and public officials regularly refer them to mediation and often they are successfully resolved. Issues include truancy, juvenile delinquency, separation, divorce, child custody, child support, visitation, spousal support, financial settlement, and property distribution. By the very interpersonal nature of these issues emotions are strong and intense. Accordingly, training and expertise in this field of mediation is required. Most family mediations include important constituents, including children, grandparents, new partners, and childcare givers. Each of these constituents has a stake in the outcome and their interests, such as they are known, should be taken into consideration. Of course, the interests of children are a priority; the court's primary concern is that any mediated agreement guarantees their welfare.

Neutrals who mediate family and domestic cases are well-trained experts in family law and in the distinctive nature of such cases. Credentials for certification vary somewhat from state to state; but training typically includes knowledge of family law, knowledge of behavioral and family dynamics, the impact of conflict on parents and children, recognition of spousal and child neglect and abuse, and a general knowledge of child development. Neutrals also are trained to recognize the impact on families of culture and social dynamics, like economics and diversity. Family mediation is not an alternative but a supplement to families who need legal counsel and clinical assistance. It is, however, an attractive option many families in conflict benefit from, for several reasons: the power of participants to resolve their own conflicts, especially regarding the interest of their own children, distributing assets, and reducing emotional stress. In addition, mediation costs significantly less than litigation. Those interested may want to consult "Model Standards of Practice for Family and Divorce Mediation," a document that reflects the *National Standards for Courts Connected Dispute Resolution Programs* (1992). In addition to these standards, state and local regulations govern family mediation and neutrals.

In this chapter, many of the issues related to family and domestic mediation are briefly addressed, including, first of all, a range of definitions.

- *Guardian ad litem*: a legal guardian, often an attorney, appointed by the court to represent children and act on behalf of their best interests. Accordingly, this person, like a parent, has access to all information relevant to the case, but does not have the right to appeal.
- *Physical (residential) custody*: the parent or parents or guardian with whom a child resides most of the time. Each state also establishes criteria for determining *joint physical custody* in which the child resides each year with both parents for a substantial amount of time. For example, if a child resides with each parent at least 100 days out of a year, that scenario might constitute joint physical custody.
- *Legal custody*: the parent(s) responsible for making major decisions regarding the child's welfare. *Sole legal custody* is when one parent is authorized, *joint legal custody* is when both parents equally are authorized, to make these decisions. Major decisions include childcare, physical and mental health, counseling, school, religion, and extracurricular activities like clubs and athletics. Legally, joint custody differs in each state according to its particular statutes.
- *Visitation*: the time a child spends with a particular parent, especially when physical custody is solely with the other parent. In most states parents, including grandparents, have a legal right to "visit" their child unless denied for cause by a court. Visitation rights may include time during the week, a weekend, alternative or split holidays, birthdays, vacations, and so on.
- *Child support*: money paid to the custodial parent (or agency supporting that parent) that is used for the needs of a child and is not tax deductible. *Shared child support* acknowledges the degree of support required of each parent in order to meet the child's needs. Most states establish a formula and scale for determining the proportionate child support required of each parent (see figure 7.1). This worksheet typically factors gross monthly income of each parent, days per year of residential custody, medical costs, childcare costs, etc.

Shared Custody Child Support Guideline Worksheet: An Example

Date: 6/22/2014   Worksheet for: Mary Davis and Jack Davis

A. Gross Income of Parties   **Mother**   **Father**

    1. Monthly Gross Income: of each Party: $_____$ $_____$
    2. Combined Gross Income: $_____$
    3. Each Party's % of Combined Gross Income: %_____   %_____
    4. Number of children: _____   Ages of children:_____

B. Support Need of Children

    1. Child support from Guideline Table (See figure 7.3)$_____$
    2. Total Shared Support=Guideline Support X 1.25 $_____$
    3. Total Days in year children reside with   Mother_____   Father_____
        each parent:
    4. Each Parent's Custody Share (%)   Mother%_____   Father%_____
        (% of 365 total days in year)

C. Support Obligation of Father

    1. Basic support obligation to Mother: $_____$ (Line B4 X Line B2)
    2. Work-related childcare costs of Mother $_____$
    3. Health insurance paid by Mother $_____$
    4. Sum of 1, 2, and 3= Total support $_____$

    5. **Father's Support Obligation** $_____$ (Line C4 X Line A3)

D. Support Obligation of Mother

    1. Basic support obligation to Father $_____$ (Line B4 X Line B2)
    2. Work-related childcare costs to Father $_____$
    3. Health insurance paid by Father $_____$
    4. Sum of 1, 2, and 3 $_____$

    5. **Mother's Support Obligation** $_____$ (Line D4 X Line A3)

E. Net Support Payable Monthly by One Parent to the Other
    (Subtract the **Lower Obligation** from **Higher Obligation** $_____$

Submitted by_____

Figure 7.1.   Custody Worksheet / Practice I

Shared Custody Child Support Guideline Worksheet: An Example

Date: 6/22/2014   Worksheet for: Mary Davis and Jack Davis

A. Gross Income of Parties   **Mother**   **Father**

   1. Monthly Gross Income: of each Party: $ 2,300___ $ 5,400_____
   2. Combined Gross Income: $_____
   3. Each Party's % of Combined Gross Income: %_____   %_____
   4. Number of children: __2___   Ages of children:__7 & 9_____

B. Support Need of Children

   1. Child support from Guideline Table (See figure 7.3) $_____
   2. Total Shared Support=Guideline Support X 1.25 $_____
   3. Total Days in year children reside with   Mother_219_   Father_146_
     each parent:
   4. Each Parent's Custody Share (%)   Mother%_____   Father%_____
     (% of 365 total days in year)

C. Support Obligation of Father

   1. Basic support obligation to Mother: $_____   (Line B4 X Line B2)
   2. Work-related childcare costs of Mother $__210_____
   4. Health insurance paid by Mother $__0_____
   4. Sum of 1, 2, and 3= Total support $_____

   5. Father's Support Obligation $_____   (Line C4 X Line A3)

D. Support Obligation of Mother

   1. Basic support obligation to Father $_____   (Line B4 X Line B2)
   2. Work-related childcare costs to Father $___160_____
   3. Health insurance paid by Father $___140_____
   4. Sum of 1, 2, and 3 $_____

   5. Mother's Support Obligation $_____   (Line D4 X Line A3)

E. Net Support Payable Monthly by One Parent to the Other
   (Subtract the **Lower Obligation** from **Higher Obligation** $_____

Submitted by:_____

Figure 7.2.   Custody Worksheet / Practice II

- *Spousal support*: money paid to an (ex)spouse with a lower income. It is tax deductible for the paying spouse and taxable income for the recipient parent.

The worksheets shown in figure 7.1 and 7.2 are examples of how child support might be determined in a case of joint legal custody.

A Shared Custody Child Support worksheet is *only* a guideline. For mediation agreements that include custody arrangements this worksheet is always included and submitted to the court. However, an agreement signed by the disputants does not have to strictly abide by the calculated net support obligation identified by this form; it is only a guideline. But if there are any proposed changes to or deviations from this obligation, the court will want to know what the changes are; it is primarily interested in certifying that the support needs of children are guaranteed by responsible parties.

DOMESTIC ABUSE

The most important issue in family mediation is the reality and/or threat of violence, abuse, and neglect. Abuse directed toward a spouse or child or senior or oneself usually constitutes an exemption from or termination of mediation. For the courts and for mediation safety is above all else. "[E]xemption from family mediation is necessary because spousal abuse is pervasive in our [American] society. Abuse is estimated to occur in 30 percent of marriages. Most victims of abuse are women; only 5 percent of reported spouse abuse victims are men. [Moreover,] mediation in domestic relations cases raises concerns about safety, because studies find more abuse after mediation sessions than after trials."[1] What constitutes "domestic violence," of course, varies from state to state and in local jurisdictions; but in most it includes conditions in which a person suffers actual physical abuse, emotional or psychological abuse, verbal abuse, sexual abuse, drug or alcohol abuse, even "economic abuse," or when there is "good cause" for believing such abuse has occurred. Some states permit mediation if all parties, including the neutral and court, are fully aware of the history of abuse and all parties agree to mediation. This is why neutrals need to be fully trained in family law; each state establishes statutory exemptions from mediation and clear guidelines for determining "good cause" for exemption from mediation.

Screening for domestic abuse, accordingly, is of utmost importance. To determine whether there is a "culture of abuse" that begs exemption, at least three phenomena should be considered: (1) there is some actual abuse, physical, emotional, sexual, or psychological; (2) there is some pattern of domination and control by the perpetrator; and (3) the victim typically tries to hide, deny, or minimize abuse.[2] If the screener determines that there is "good cause" for suspecting a pattern of abuse, then mediation is usually not a viable option; it is unlikely, under such conditions of intimidation and fear, that mediation and negotiation could occur with fairness and equal power. Exempting parties from mediation based on screening is preferable but not always possible; sometimes the level and intensity of abuse only becomes evident to the neutral during the mediation session itself. In such cases the neutral should caucus with each party and then immediately terminate the session. Safety and balance of power should always be a priority in mediation.

PROPERTY: MATERIAL AND FINANCIAL

The process and complexity of separation and divorce is complicated by the extent of the parties' property, both material and financial. Neutrals trained in family mediation will be familiar with laws stipulating ways in which property is distributed. Most states, for example, stipulate how insurance policies and pensions and investments are divided and distributed. The checklist of issues provided in figure 7.4 is a helpful guide.

Child Support Guidelines
(Partial table)

Combined Monthly Gross Income	One Child	Two Children	Three Children	Etc.
3000	445	691	866	
3050	450	699	876	
3100	461	715	896	
/				
/				
/				
/				
/				
/				
/				
/				
/				
7000	848	1315	1644	
7050	852	1320	1651	
7100	855	1325	1658	
7150	859	1331	1665	
7200	862	1336	1671	
7250	866	1341	1678	
7300	870	1347	1685	
7350	873	1352	1692	
7400	877	1358	1698	
7450	880	1363	1705	
7500	884	1368	1712	
7550	887	1374	1719	
7600	891	1379	1725	
7650	895	1384	1732	
7700	898	1390	1739	
7750	902	1395	1746	
7800	905	1400	1753	
7850	908	1405	1758	
/				
/				
//				

Figure 7.3. Child Support Guidelines

Checklist for Family Mediation

Children

Basic Information
__Complete names & SSN
__Children's names, Age, SSN

Child Custody/Parenting
__Custody: legal
__Physician/medical treatment
__Education/schools
__Childcare
__Extracurricular activities
__Discipline/behavior standards
__Religion

Residential/Visitation
__Custody: physical
__Visitation
__Holidays/special days
__Vacation
__Media interaction
__Relocation

Child Support/Expenses
__Payment/how/when
__Life insurance beneficiaries
__Tax exemptions
__Health insurance
__Co-pays/other medical expenses
__College/vocational expenses

Spouses

Spouses Expenses
__Spousal support
__Health insurance

Property/Debts
__Incomes
__Residence/land
__Household furnishings
__Vehicles/insurance
__Bank accounts
__Credit cards/debt
__Anticipated expenses

Separation/Divorce
__Dates: marriage/separation
__Reconciliation
__Communication
__Dating/partners
__Divorce
__Legal expenses
__Name change

Expenses/Resources
__Education/training
__Life insurance
__Taxes/payment/refunds
__Investments/stocks/assets
__Bankruptcy/liabilities
__Inheritance

Figure 7.4. Checklist for Family Mediation

INQUIRY AND REFLECTION EXERCISES

1. Using a calculator, complete the Shared Child Support form. The worksheet in figure 7.2 can be used to practice with your mediation role-play team. The Child Support Guidelines appear in figure 7.3.

2. Insofar as they are available, access your State Supreme Court website online and find out what your home state's divorce guidelines are for screening for domestic abuse and for exempting a case from mediation (if those guidelines are available).

3. Insofar as they are available, access your State Supreme Court website online and find out what your home state's divorce guidelines are for distributing insurance policies, pensions, and other investments.

NOTES

1. "Family Mediation: Screening for Domestic Abuse." http://www.law.fsu.edu/journals/lawreview/issues/231/gerencse.html, p. 4.
   2. *Ibid.*, pp. 5–6.

8

Business and Organizational Mediation

PRINCIPLED NEGOTIATION

Most people experience conflict not just in family life but also in professional life. Whenever people organize themselves for the purpose of achieving a common goal, tensions and conflicts are inevitable. The basic principles and values of mediation, its stages and skills, are largely the same in business as in any other sphere of life; and yet there are certain distinctive applications that neutrals are trained to manage. The book that revolutionized conflict resolution, especially in business communities, was written in 1981 by Roger Fisher and William L. Ury in conjunction with the Harvard Negotiation Project titled *Getting to Yes: Negotiating Agreement Without Giving In.*[1] Fisher and Ury advocate a method called "principled negotiation" based on five propositions:

1. "Separate the people from the problem." Every conflict consists of two dimensions—one relational and the other substantial. There is, on the one hand, the parties' attitudes and prejudices toward each other, which is not the focus of negotiation; there is, on the other hand, the interests and needs of each party that lend themselves to negotiated agreement. One's negative feelings about and dislike for the other party are not the same as the common interests and issues to be resolved. Keeping these two dimensions distinct and focusing on the latter is crucial for achieving success.
2. "Focus on interests, not positions." Closely related is another distinction, between the positions toward issues that one takes and the actual issues and concerns themselves. The process of clarifying and identifying compatible interests from opposing positions different parties take on those issues is again important for resolution to take place.

3. "Invent options for mutual gain." Generating possible options freely through brainstorming is sometimes difficult, because a disputant is often suspicious of the other party's suggestions, and often defensive, and focused on "Getting what I want" instead of "Getting what we need." Imagining new and different options may require parties, for a time, to bracket judgment and evaluation.

4. "Insist on using objective criteria." After generating a variety of possible solutions, the parties can then evaluate them based on fair and mutually beneficial outcomes (win/win). Instead of focusing on how much one is giving up to the other person, focus on how each party is contributing on principle to constructing a mutually fair solution.

5. "Know your BATNA (Best Alternative to Negotiated Agreement)." Each party should consider what course of action they are realistically willing and able to undertake, if negotiation is not successful.

These five elements of principled negotiation in one form or another have been examined in part II of this book. Along with the mediation process and skilled neutrals, they represent an approach that is powerful and effective in resolving conflict in a wide variety of organizational venues: conflicts arising with those who make policy, to those who administer policy, to those who deliver and implement policy.

It is worth noting that in a more recent, supplemental study to *Getting to Yes*, five motivational "core concerns" of principled negotiation are identified and examined. What primarily motivates people, Fisher and Shapiro discover, are appreciation, affiliation, autonomy, status, and role. Although these motivations may contribute to conflict, they are also powerful prompts for establishing common ground and resolving conflict.[2] They are catalysts that inspire disputants to desire resolution and a work environment conducive to collaboration and cooperation.

WORKPLACE CONFLICT AND PRODUCTIVITY

Perhaps the primary deficit of conflict in the workplace is its cost, the loss of productivity and profits. In an article posted by *The Financial Manager* (2006),[3] the costs to businesses associated with conflict include:

- *Reduced productivity* resulting from personnel involved both directly and indirectly in conflict. Estimated losses of productivity by managers, due to conflict among team members, range as high as 30 to 40 percent.
- Surveys show that workplace conflict is the leading cause of employee *turnover* (other than downsizing, mergers, and restructuring) and that

turnover is expensive; replacing an employee can cost up to 150 percent of annual salary.

- Workplace conflict often generates bad business decisions. "Personal fears, antagonisms, and biases related to conflict can prevent or undermine sound business *decisionmaking*." Although the results are somewhat elusive, the poor decisionmaking that results from managerial conflict (marketing and sales, for example) is costly to an organization, in terms of productivity, time, and energy.

Two organizational formulas for calculating the costs of conflict are as follows, according to *The Financial Manager*:[4]

Reduced Productivity=
Number of employees affected by conflict × daily hours lost × average hourly wage × 250[5]

Employee turnover resulting from conflict=
Number of employees lost × annual salary × 1.5

Managers and CFOs usually do not think of costs associated with workplace conflicts, although at least some of the costs resulting from turnover is often accounted for. The bad news, then, is that conflicts are costly for businesses; the good news is that conflicts can be reduced if not prevented, and they can be resolved.

Recommendations for dealing with conflicts in the workplace and for reducing their impact on financial and human resources are based on common sense. The most important recommendation, perhaps, is (1) to train administrators and managers in the art of conflict resolution. This is not so much for the purpose of themselves resolving conflict, although that may occur, but for the purpose of nurturing in managers a sensitivity for recognizing early on in its development the reality of conflict and its sources. Once acknowledged, (2) experienced neutrals should be retained to assist in mediating conflicts before they damage personnel and productivity. In this way productivity can be sustained and turnover reduced. A common mistake in the workplace is hesitation and procrastination; managers allow conflicts to take root and develop and gain a great deal of momentum, so that even when some official and formal action is taken, it is too late: productivity has already fallen and the conflict is beyond repair. In addition, a business should (3) train and maintain a literate workforce; workshops in conflict and conflict resolution should be a vital part of a company's professional training plan. Since the potential for conflict is as present in a workplace as productivity, and since productivity can be damaged by conflict, it is simply good business sense to prepare employees for dealing with interpersonal conflict. Finally, (4) employees need to know specifically "who to go to" when they are feeling tension with a colleague or are upset with the behavior of others, including supervisors, or upset with the nature and structure of their work. Human resource officers may function in this way, or some other person who is equipped to listen and set in motion a process that candidly deals with employees' concerns. Identifying mentors for new employees is another option. Mentors should be selected from outside the new employee's department, if possible, so that the new hire can speak candidly about any concerns including tensions with departmental colleagues. Making available to employees a Conflict Resolution form (like the one in figure 8.1) may encourage reticent workers to more readily initiate the process toward resolving conflict instead of "putting up with it" until it is too late.

The more easily accessible the resources for resolving conflict, the more likely it is that employees will initiate the process for doing so.

Conflict in the workplace, of course, occurs at all levels of organization, "and . . . its effects are more costly the higher you go. . . . [Indeed,] poor communication and impaired decision-making at this higher level of management can cost the company far more than just near-term productivity reductions. It can lead to missed opportunities and unaddressed threats that can change the fundamental health of the organization."[6] It is incumbent on the leaders in any company, then, to include a plan for conflict management and to cultivate a culture of openness and honesty at all levels, so that tensions and conflicts can be addressed before they take root and damage productivity and employee morale.

ORGANIZATIONAL CONFLICT

Most people experience not only interpersonal conflicts but also intergroup conflict, collective conflict originating in the dynamics of an organization, whether professional, political, religious, or non-profit. In such instances, the process of mediation and the role of a neutral is roughly the same as for individual, interpersonal conflict resolution. However, intergroup, aggregate conflict has distinct concerns and challenges that are addressed here. Indeed, when people organize themselves socially several issues typically arise, including (1) Whose voice represents the voice of the whole? (2) How will that representative voice be selected? (3) What views will that voice articulate? And (4) How are those views selected and determined? There is no single method or way of addressing each of these questions, but to successfully resolve organizational conflict, the group needs to address them.

Request for Conflict Resolution

Personal Information

Name:_____   Date:_____

Position:_____

Department/Section:_____

Nature of the Conflict

Name of Other Party or Parties:_____

_____

Brief Description of Conflict: Issues and Interests:

Signature:_____

Figure 8.1.   Request for Conflict Resolution

1. The person or persons who represent an aggregate, however they are selected, need to be articulate, well-informed, and generally respected by its members. By "articulate" I mean one who is able to verbalize complex issues and ideas in a simple, clear, and logical/organized fashion; by "informed" I mean someone who has knowledge of the history of the issues and concerns, and who has sufficient experience in the organization to speak with some authority about them; and by "respected" I mean a person of integrity and honor in the eyes not only of peers but of management as well. The best representative voice, in other words, is not necessarily the most vocal or assertive person.

2. The process by which a representative voice is selected may be inherent in the structure of the group itself. That is, the director or supervisor or chair of a department may be the voice best suited to the role; but maybe not. Sometimes they are "distant" from the experiences and issues that concern the aggregate; a better voice may be from among the workers themselves. Moreover, the conflict itself may be between that supervisor, and the management concerns she represents, and the aggregate. Hence, a different voice from among the workers needs to be selected. This may be accomplished variously: a volunteer, popular vote, or some other means of consensus. In short, the selected person needs the support of those she represents and the aggregate needs the representative to be one who they see as reliable and in whom they have confidence.

3. Once the representative voice is selected, substantive questions arise: What are the issues and concerns the aggregate wishes their representative to articulate and advocate? Clearly the members of the group themselves need to collaborate and decide what issues are most important to them and what priority weight to confer on each of them. Rarely is there a single, individual issue that is unrelated to others; tensions with a supervisor usually involve several issues, like personality, working conditions, adequate material and human resources, project deadlines, lack of clear objectives, etc. The group should be clear about those issues that most concern them and what they would like to accomplish in mediation.

4. The process by which these substantive issues are determined by the aggregate should be transparent and collaborative; all members should have equal say and input. Group meetings and discussions are crucial to success; but given the reality of some personalities that are timid and reserved, soliciting written comments is also an important way of developing a comprehensive perspective that truly represents the entire group. Without adequate group collaboration the selected voice is unlikely to be representative.

As indicated throughout this chapter, resolving conflict early and often yields great benefits for businesses and organizations; those benefits include the welfare and retention of employees, efficiency of the workforce, and increased productivity and profit.

SMALL CLAIMS MEDIATION

One kind of dispute that lends itself to successful mediation is collected under the category of "small claims," as in "small claims court." Indeed, small claims constitute a significant slice of cases mediated by neutrals and mediation centers, and training in small claims mediation is usually available from training centers. Small claims include disputes between friends, neighbors, customers, consumers, and partners; a sample list of issues includes:

- land lord/tenant—eviction, security deposit
- business/customer complaint
- neighbors—property disputes, encroachment of trees, bushes; noise, animals, other disturbances
- breach of contract/warranty—construction, services, liability
- clinician/provider/patient/consumer
- debt collection/repaying loans—suing/being sued
- real estate—homeowners association
- personal injury—traffic accidents

Such disputes are managed in the same way as other conflicts; a neutral facilitates the steps of the mediation process, in expectation of resolving most conflicts. Neutrals are trained in relevant small claims laws and codes, which govern mediated agreements just as in litigated agreements.

INQUIRY AND REFLECTION EXERCISES

1. Recall the personal conflict you described in chapters 1, 2, and 3. Explain the difference between the "interests" in that conflict and the "positions" taken by each of the disputants.

2. Think of a group or organization you were/are a part of. Describe an aggregate conflict, either internal or external, that distracted the group from working toward its goals. What kind of "conflict style" (avoidance, competing, etc.) did the group use in dealing with the conflict? How was it resolved or why was it not resolved?

3. Use the formula for "reduced productivity" to calculate the cost of conflict when the number of employees affected is five; the number of work hours lost daily is 2½; and the average hourly wage is $18.75.

4. Use the formula for "turnover" to calculate the cost of conflict when the number of employees lost is two and the average annual salary is $42,000.

5. Form several groups from among class members (ten or more people in an aggregate). As a group accomplish the four steps set forth in the section "Organizational Conflict" by selecting one of the following aggregate scenarios.

Scenario One: Your aggregate consists of a group of concerned college students whose purpose is to bring to the Director of Student Life a constellation of issues that the group would like to discuss and address by implementing specific solutions upon which the aggregate agrees.

Scenario Two: Your aggregate consists of a group of progressive environmentalists whose purpose is to bring to the local city government specific solutions to issues the group has identified.

Scenario Three: Your aggregate consists of a group of concerned Tea Party advocates whose purpose is to bring to local city government certain issues that you consider a matter of private and personal freedom that government should have no business interfering with.

NOTES

1. Fisher, Roger & Ury, William. *Getting to Yes: Negotiating Agreement Without Giving In* (New York: Penguin Group, 1981).
2. R. Fisher & D. Shapiro, *Beyond Reason: Using Emotions as You Negotiate* (New York: Viking Press, 2005).
3. http://www.bmcassociates.com/resources/articles/conflict-management/print.
4. *Ibid.*, 4.
5. The approximate number of workdays in a year's time.
6. http://www.bmcassociates.com/resources/articles/conflict-management/print, 5.

9

Criminal Justice and Mediation

RE-ENFRANCHISING VICTIMS

Gradually, globally, over the past forty years or so, a modern restorative justice movement has emerged as a supplement, if not alternative, to conventional systems of retributive justice and rehabilitation services. Something like restorative justice, however, has deep historical and cultural roots in many traditional, indigenous cultures. Some scholars insist that it was even a dominant model for centuries.[1] Be that as it may, modern criminal justice systems have tended to maximize retributive over restorative systems. From early childhood we are socialized to make not only judgments regarding right and wrong but judgments regarding just and unjust punishments. Our criminal justice systems presuppose, often uncritically, that justice necessarily requires retribution and little more. Indeed, the retributive model of justice is so thoroughly woven into the fabric of societies that it is often difficult to envision the viability of any other model.

Recall from our discussion in chapter 1 that one fundamental difference between retributive and restorative justice is the kind of relationship on which each focuses: whereas retribution focuses on the relationship between offender(s) and the law/state, restorative justice focuses on the relationship between offender(s) and victim(s). As a means of restoring this latter relationship, restorative justice draws on the assumptions, values, principles, and processes of mediation and negotiation. To compensate for the fact that current criminal justice systems assume that crime is primarily an offense against the state and law, restorative systems focus on crime as an offense against persons, neighborhoods, and communities. In the context of a dominant retributive system, restorative justice is revolutionary. It asks different questions from those asked by retributive justice. It is not primarily interested in "what should be done to the offender, but how the harm (caused by a crime) can be repaired. This is what distinguishes it from a punitive justice approach, and also from the rehabilitative perspective."[2] Accordingly, restorative justice must deal with different problems and do so in different ways that typically include negotiation and mediation procedures. Following the lead of the United Nations' *Handbook for Restorative Justice Programmes* (2006), instead of a definition of restorative justice, I offer a constellation of fundamental traits and principles:

1. Reconciliation: The aim of restorative justice is not punitive as in most current criminal systems; instead its aim is to reconcile through a process of negotiation and mediation the offender and offended, the criminal and victim. It assumes that crime is fundamentally an offense that shatters to some degree human dignity and community, and assumes that it is desirable to heal and restore those relationships.
2. Collaboration: The process of restorative justice requires collaboration and cooperation between offender and offended, and often achieves outcomes that are satisfactory for both offender and offended. In contrast retributive justice is adversarial in nature, requiring participants to compete legally for self-interested and often incorrigible outcomes.
3. Voluntary and Inclusive: Participation in a restorative justice process is available to any and all offenders. Even criminals who have committed gross felonies may participate, even though participating is generally not a substitute for the punitive measures enforced by retributive justice. For restorative justice to succeed, participation is and must be voluntary; both offender and offended must voluntarily agree to participate.
4. Empowerment: Restorative justice re-enfranchises and empowers victim(s), who a retributive system typically ignores. Victims should have a stake in the criminal justice process and should participate in the direction and outcomes of criminal justice. Restorative justice, in other words, takes into account the needs and interests of victims in a way retributive justice does not and cannot.
5. Responsibility: Restorative justice requires offenders to assume personal and moral responsibility for the offense(s) and crimes(s) committed. Offenders must be willing to "face up" to both their crimes and to the persons offended, and be willing to seek amends and reparations for their behavior.
6. Community: Restorative justice assumes that the well-being of victims is of utmost importance and that victims are never simply or only an individual person, but a neighborhood, a community, a family, a soci-

ety, a group, or "conference." Theft, rape, murder, fraud, and assault are liable to offend and disrupt the civility and interpersonal tranquility of communities of people, not just single individuals.

7. Mediation: Restorative justice is an application of mediation and its values to systems of criminal justice. It assumes that reconciliation between offenders and offended is possible and plausible through the peacebuilding process of negotiation/mediation. Ordinarily, a neutral mediator manages the procedural steps of a mediated process in order to resolve conflicts and heal relationships between offender and offended.

8. Confidentiality: As in all mediation, the restorative justice process is confidential. Legally this means that the courts do not have access to the substance of the mediation; only access to the official, mediated agreement, which is submitted to the court for its evaluation.

9. Safety: Restorative justice guarantees a safe, secure environment for offender and offended to express feelings and perspectives regarding injuries and harm, and to do so without fear of reprisals. In the safety of a mediated context, genuine healing and closure can occur.

Many key transformative values underlie these principles. A variety of official international human rights agreements reflect many of the values underwriting restorative justice:[3] empathy and compassion, forgiveness, human dignity; tend to heal injury and harm, and repair broken relationships including personal, communal, and civic. Such agreements restore property and environment, emotional stability, freedom and self-determination, and a sense of civic duty and interpersonal responsibility.

CRIMINAL JUSTICE SYSTEMS

Restorative justice is increasingly present in courtrooms and prisons, not just in North America but throughout the world. Public and political voices are calling for reform of criminal justice systems—police, courts, sentencing, and prisons. Restorative justice is poised to be a crucial part of those reforms. Judges, prosecutors, defense attorneys, probation officers, and case workers are increasingly involved in considering, implementing, and monitoring it. Many professionals as well as citizens are enthusiastic about this alternative supplement to conventional retributive systems. But what conditions, then, trigger a restorative, transformative approach to justice, and how does such a process begin?

Those who typically initiate the restorative process, not surprisingly, are police, judges, lawyers, counselors, case managers, family members, even criminals and victims. Some restorative justice enthusiasts insist that any crime might lend itself to restorative procedures; others consider certain kinds of crimes more suitable for it than other crimes. Some scholars have developed something called a "Regulatory Pyramid" as a means for solving "the puzzle of when to punish [retribution] and when to persuade [restore]."[4] In fact, in many instances both retributive and restorative measures may be applied for a single crime. In cases of rape, for example, the criminal may participate in a restorative procedure while also serving prison time.

But when and why might courts recommend restorative instead of retributive measures as a way of dealing with crime? On what bases might restorative justice supplant instead of merely supplement retributive justice? Criteria include non-violent crime, first-time offenders, and juvenile offenders. Indeed, current restorative justice programs originated primarily for juvenile delinquents, which continues as a primary group that is likely to benefit from restorative measures. "When restorative justice is considered in most political jurisdictions, youth are typically its first intended targets. . . . Since young people are still in a process of formation, they are considered malleable and open to change. It is at this point that we can seek to halt their initial 'drift' (Matza 1990)"[5] and redirect them toward constructive, civil, acceptable ways of living in society. In such cases, the restorative sessions are generally between two groups—the juvenile and parents on the one hand, and victim and community on the other, with court certified mediators presiding.

Restorative justice embraces a wide range of criminal cases, from small, petty misdemeanors to massive, collective, national tragedies. Consider two cases, one on either end of this crime/criminal spectrum. (1) Two teenagers, Ian, age 16, and Caitrin, 17, spray the public wall of an underpass with graffiti, including offensive curse words. Both are from middle class families and are students at Middletown High School, where both excel at art and design classes. Ian's father is a pastor of a local Baptist church and Caitrin's mother is on city council. Defacing public property is a misdemeanor and typically requires detention in a juvenile facility. In addition, Ian and Caitrin bullied, threatened, and beat up a peer, Kevin, who happened to observe them defacing the wall. All parties agreed to meet for a restorative justice session; the parties included Ian, Caitrin, and their parents, Kevin and his parents, two members of city council, representing the city and its concern for public safety/public property, and a mediator. Imagine what kind of issues and resolutions this session might yield.

As it happened, the guided, mediated session yielded a constructive and innovative agreement. All parties submitted their issues and concerns and struggled through several sessions to satisfy the needs of all parties. All agreed that to incarcerate Ian and Caitrin would be counter-productive and should not be pursued. Kevin and his parents agreed (a) that Ian and Caitrin should submit in writing a letter of apology to Kevin, and (b) pay for Kevin's physician and medical bills. The agreement with the city, included (a) a letter of apology to the city council; included in the discussion was possibly a letter of apology from Ian and Caitrin to be published in the local paper; that was rejected as too publicly humiliating; (b) an agreement to remove the graffiti from the wall, at their own expense; (c) organize the high school art class to paint "respectable and approved murals" on the walls of several public underpasses around town; and (d) twenty hours each of volunteering at the local food bank.

(2) Consider the Truth and Reconciliation Commission in South Africa, which originated in 1995 as an effort to address the national tragedy of apartheid and restore mutual respect and civility between criminals and victims. The two parties in conflict, in this case, were the black victims of apartheid (who numbered in the thousands), on the one hand, and the perpetrators of apartheid, on the other hand, including the government of South Africa, the apartheid system it sustained, many of its employees, including government, police, and military personnel, and citizens protected by the government's apartheid system. The apartheid system in South Africa parallels the segregation codified by Jim Crow laws in the United States. "Apartheid" is an Afrikaan word meaning "separateness" or "segregation" based on racial identity. It was a system of racial segregation in South Africa legally enforced by the National Party that governed from 1948–1994. The rights and freedoms of black South Africans and other minorities were severely restricted or denied, including the right to form associations, the right to citizenship, the right to live where and as one chooses, the right to freedom of movement and employment, along with segregated public spaces (beaches), education, medical care, and so on, all of which were inferior to those services available to the white population. Not surprisingly, apartheid generated internal resistance movements and violence, and international protests and boycotts. After the abolition of apartheid, the newly elected democratic government initiated a Truth and Reconciliation Commission. It was a kind of court formed to treat the criminals involved in apartheid according to the principles and values of restorative justice. Indeed, the neutral third party mediator was "a juristic person . . . known as the Truth and Reconciliation Commission,"[6] with Archbishop Desmond Tutu as its chair, appointed by the newly elected democratic government and its president Nelson Mandela. The mandate and objectives of the Commission embody many of the values and principles and techniques of the Transformation Model, of mediation and restorative justice.

The explicit **aim** of the Commission is to address "gross violations of human rights" in South Africa, including torture and murder; to seek reconciliation between offenders and victims; to encourage "understanding but not . . . vengeance," and ultimately to cultivate national unity.[7] The **means** by which this aim is addressed include (a) face-to-face "engagement" between offenders and offended, (b) amnesty for offenders "who make full disclosure of all the relevant facts relating to acts associated with [apartheid]," and (c) reparations for the victims. The **process** for achieving this aim and implementing these means is the Commission itself, which as "a juristic person" functions as a neutral mediator, assisting offenders and offended in negotiating amnesty and policies for granting reparations. In so doing, the Commission embodies values and principles of transformation and the Transformation Model. For example, the Commission focuses on collecting "relevant facts" regarding violations of human rights, "the nature, causes, and extent of gross violations of human rights," "the identity [and responsibility] of all persons, authorities, institutions and organisations involved in such violations," and granting amnesty, granting fair reparations, and creating just resolutions and agreements regarding "institutions conducive to a stable and fair society."[8] Although this Commission encountered problems and its successes are perhaps more modest than desirable, nevertheless, its successes demonstrate that peaceful transformation through mediation is relevant to resolving not only local, individual cases of criminal justice, but also massive national and international conflicts.

BENEFITS OF RESTORATIVE JUSTICE

A legitimate question lingers: "To what extent does restorative justice 'work'?" Answering questions of this sort is not easy, partly because it is difficult to establish objective criteria for what counts as "working." However, studies have been conducted that establish a trajectory of empirical evidence regarding the effectiveness of restorative justice. John Braithwaite, in his book *Restorative Justice and Responsive Regulation*, does us the favor of summarizing much of this evidence and in doing so answers the above question in the affirmative. The following encapsulates his summary in chapter 3 titled "Does Restorative Justice Work?" Braithwaite organizes his summary around three foci:

1. Restorative justice restores and satisfies victims better than existing criminal justice practices.

    Based on "a welter of studies reviewed" there is "comparatively high victim approval of their restorative justice experiences, though often lower levels of approval than one finds among other participants in the process,"[9] such as offenders and community representatives. Satisfaction is high for all parties who participate in restorative justice measures, in other words, but higher among offenders and community representatives. Nevertheless, for victims whose cases were resolved in court, for example, more than half said they would harm their assailant if they had a chance, compared with only 7 percent of those whose cases were resolved through restorative justice programs.

2. Restorative justice restores and satisfies offenders better than existing criminal justice practices.

   Studies find that offender satisfaction is quite high for those whose cases were resolved through restorative justice programs. Based on studies "The evidence of offenders being restored in the sense of desisting from criminal conduct is extremely encouraging. . . ."[10] Indeed, one study found "mediation recidivism to be one-third lower than court recidivism."[11] Moreover, based on an analysis of thirty-four program samples, researchers found that "offender perception of both fairness and satisfaction was highest for fully restorative programs and lowest for nonrestorative programs."[12] Outcomes of restorative justice endeavors, in other words, yield greater satisfaction for offenders than do nonrestorative, retributive programs.

3. Restorative justice restores and satisfies communities better than existing criminal justice practices.

The makeup and extent of "community" in restorative justice sessions varies according to each case. A community may consist of the family of the victim, the extended family, a neighborhood, a community organization, a clique of friends, any "micro-community," and so on. Sometimes such restorative sessions are referred to as "conferences" or "healing circles." Incorporating an extended community into the restorative session is important not only because many are impacted by crime, but also because many are needed to restore and reconcile offender and offended. Including extended family in a restorative session is important, for example, when rape is an ongoing, trans-generational tragedy. The intent is not only to reduce the likelihood of repeating rape in the extended family, but also finding and building on a family strength that might enhance healthy instead of abusive relationships.[13]

Studies of community engagement in restorative justice sessions indicate several tentative trends:[14] (1) that offenders, victims, and police express high degrees (over 90 percent for all participants) of satisfaction (e.g., Pennell and Burford, 1995); (2) that parents of offenders are "more satisfied (97 percent) and more likely to believe that justice has been fair (97 percent) than in cases that went to court" (McCold and Wachetel, 1998); (3) "evidence is overwhelming that where communities show strong social support [for restorative justice], criminality is less" (Cullen 1994; Chamlin and Cochran 1997). Finally, (4) Braithwaite argues that restorative justice programs enhance at a grass roots level democratic values, by encouraging communities to assume responsibility for criminal behavior, for healing the relationship between criminal, victim, and community, and for building the kind of community in which crime is less likely to occur.

In conclusion, research tends to show in a variety of ways that restorative justice programs are beneficial to addressing criminal justice concerns; they are beneficial for offender, victim, and community alike; they satisfy all participating parties at a significantly higher rate than conventional criminal justice practices. Accordingly, increasing the quality and reach of such programs is crucial for reforming current retributive and rehabilitative systems of justice.

INQUIRY AND REFLECTION EXERCISES

1. Reread and review the discussion of retributive and restorative justice in chapter 1 (pages 7–9).

2. How would you evaluate the restorative quality of the agreement (pages 102–3) for the case of Ian and Caitrin? Strengths? Weaknesses? How might you change it? What would you add or subtract? Do you think the measures of the agreement are relevant to the nature of the crimes and adequate and fair? Explain why and why not.

3. If you are in charge, what criticisms and restrictions would you place on the practice of restorative justice in a criminal justice system?

4. As a mediator participating in a restorative justice case, what would you imagine/conceive a fair and sensible resolution to be in the following case? Instead of incarceration, what solution do you think the parties in dispute might reasonably agree to and why? Use the Conflict Grid to organize issues, facts, and possible solutions:

    Stephen is age fifteen. He lives with his mother, who is single, and a sister. The family struggles with finances—paying for rent, utilities, food, etc., and benefit from food stamps (Supplemental Nutrition Assistance Program). He loves his family and wants to contribute to finances. He has no criminal record; only several truancy difficulties and encounters with school officials. Sometimes he feels desperate to help his mother, as he did one day when walking home after dark from basketball practice. When he sees an elderly lady approaching with a purse hanging from her shoulder, he impulsively but uncharacteristically ripped the purse from her shoulders and ran, knocking her to the ground. The lady, Martha, is physically unhurt, except for a bruise on her arm. But she lost in the robbery $175, her cell phone, and credit cards. Two days later the authorities arrest Stephen. The $175 has already been spent; credit cards are retrieved, but the cell phone has been destroyed. Martha is retired and works part-time at a department store and volunteers with the American Red Cross, teaching CPR and First Aid classes. Stephen and his mother agree to meet with Martha and her husband for a mediated restorative justice session.

5. Watch the film *The Power of Forgiveness* (2004). It depicts historical instances in which criminals and victims, both individuals and groups, face up to and encounter each other in an attempt to heal and restore relationships. Select two episodes that strike you; describe the conflict and then write about the measures taken by the parties in conflict to heal and restore their relationship.

NOTES

1. See John Braithwaite's *Restorative Justice and Responsive Regulation*. London: Oxford University Press (2002), pp. 3–5.

2. Lode Walgrave, *Restorative Justice, Self-Interest and Responsible Citizenship*. Cillompton, Devon, UK: Willan Publishing (2008), p. 23.

3. These agreements include the Universal Declaration of Human Rights, the International Covenant on Civil and Political Rights, and the Declaration of Basic Principles of Justice for Victims of Crime and Abuse of Power.

4. See an example of a Regulatory Pyramid in John Braithwaite, *Restorative Justice and Responsive Regulation* (2002), pp. 30–32.

5. Andrew Woolford, *The Politics of Restorative Justice: A Critical Introduction*. Halifax and Winnipeg: Fenwood Publishing (2009), p. 123.

6. "Promotion of National Unity and Reconciliation Act 34 of 1995," chapter 2, section 2.

7. "Promotion of National Unity and Reconciliation Act 34 of 1995," ACT.

8. "Promotion of National Unity and Reconciliation Act 34 of 1995," chapter 2, section 3.

9. Braithwaite, 45.

10. *Ibid.*, 54.

11. *Ibid.*, 55.

12. *Ibid.*, 55.

13. *Ibid.*, 66.

14. *Ibid.*, 66–67.

10

International Mediation and Education

THE PROBLEM

Negotiation and mediation between nations has a long if not terribly successful history. In the fifth century BCE, Athens and Sparta, during the Peloponnesian wars, periodically struck alliances and exchanged diplomatic missions, often to no avail. Ever since, nations sometimes attempt to mediate differences, but more often than not they simply engage in armed battle. Not a day passes without news reports of international tensions and conflicts. Not only are there ongoing conflicts in all regions of the globe, the United States alone is almost continuously in conflict with one nation or terrorist organization or another. At the same time, negotiation and mediation as a means of conflict resolution are increasingly common; their success or failure sometimes determines whether protracted violence, tragedy, and loss of life occur, or reconciliation, political stability, and economic sustainability.

The Transformation Model assumes military conflict and violence are symptoms of interests and issues between nations that otherwise could be resolved peacefully, provided mediation resources are available. The causal conditions of violent conflicts:

- Border disputes are fairly common and often are the result of earlier forms of conflict, like colonization and colonial administrations. Think of India and Pakistan, Israel and Palestine, Turkey and Greece, Tibet and China, North and South Korea, Russia and Ukraine, the division of the former Yugoslavia. Sometimes borders were drawn up by colonial powers as lines on a map without respect for traditional cultural and ethnic heritages.

- Access to, delivery, and protection of natural resources are the source of many international disputes. Water resources in the Middle East, for example; or building the Keystone XL pipeline in North America, which would involve three nations—sovereign native nations, Canada, and the United States. Regulations and management of whaling, of salmon fishing, of endangered species, and the like, almost always involve the international community, since animals recognize only natural and not national boundaries.
- Immigration and refugees are an ongoing source of international conflict. Throughout the Americas, Europe, Africa, the Middle East, and Asia, political, economic, and ethnic refugees flee to neighboring countries seeking safety, stability, and sometimes citizenship. These issues generate internal national disputes as well as international conflicts that generate international resentments and hostilities.
- Economic and cultural imperialism is likely the major cause of terrorist activity globally. No doubt many in developing nations resent the cultural and economic dominance of powerful, foreign nations. Osama Bin Laden, for example, identified several sources as motivation for the terrorist activities that resulted in the tragedy of 9/11. Specifically, he identified "Western" values that undermined his version of Islamic culture and imperialism represented by the United States building a military base in his homeland Saudi Arabia.

Resolving these and other disputes peacefully through mediation resources not only would forestall the many military engagements that otherwise ignite, but would likely establish conditions and habits that promote sustainable patterns of peace among nations.

Of course, most, although not all, nations and their leaders claim they prefer peaceful resolution of conflicts. "Despite its self-evident importance, however, international mediation has not been conducted and developed in a systematic and professional manner,"[1] according to Laurie Nathan. The primary reasons for this, he says, are:

1. Insufficiently trained and experienced mediators (former heads of state, diplomats) appointed to resolve international conflicts;
2. Insufficient funding by global institutions for technical, administrative, and financial support;
3. Inadequate opportunities and organizations for training international mediators; hence an inadequate pool of expert mediators. International mediators need to be educated in the culture, languages, religions, and politics of hostile nations and regional power brokers;

4. Inadequate follow-up and assessment of international mediation cases; in order to learn lessons, adapt methods, and establish a centralized repository of available wisdom;
5. An inadequate strategy and plan for developing a uniquely international style for managing and resolving international conflicts.

Indeed, nations, the UN, and the international community have not invested sufficient human, economic, and administrative resources toward educating and preparing for sustainable peace. War and military strategies are studied assiduously and lavishly financed; not so peace and peacemaking. Furthermore, although international organizations are generally content to avert and end hostilities, they are not so eager to discover and address the underlying causes of specific conflicts. Too little study has focused on analyzing what combination of conditions make for sustainable peace among nations.

THE GLOBAL PEACE INDEX

Understanding and preventing conditions that lead to tensions, violence, and war is, of course, extremely important; but understanding and promoting conditions that lead to a sustainable peace is equally important. These two sets of causal conditions and the difficulties in measuring them are encapsulated in the Global Peace Index. This Index is the brain-child of the Institute for Economics and Peace (IEP), developed initially in 2007 in conjunction with peace experts worldwide who submit relevant data necessary for creating the Index. It now ranks 158 nations annually in terms of (a) internal conditions, such as levels of crime and violence, and (b) external conditions, such as military expenditures and engagement in actual conflicts and wars. The twenty-two criteria or "indicators" of peace,[2] according to the Index, are almost entirely related to factors of violence and war and not to conditions essential for sustaining peace. The relevant data are collected from a variety of international organizations[3] and collated by the IEP.

The Index has been criticized on at least two factors: the failure to establish positive indicators that measure conditions essential for sustainable peace; and the failure to include indicators that measure violence against women and children. More recently the Global Peace Index includes a "Positive Peace Index"; it attempts to measure attitudes and institutions and structures that seem to improve a country's peacefulness. These eight indicators of peace are well-functioning government, sound business environment, equitable distribution of resources, acceptance of the rights of minorities and others, good relations with neighbors, free flow of information, high levels of education, and low levels of corruption. As valuable and useful as this positive index is, it still mostly establishes indicators that measure the absence and prevention of problems, such as the prevention of violence, instead of measuring the presence of social conditions that promote peace. For example, the indicator "good neighbor relations" measures "personal security and trust" by assessing "levels of crime victimization, feelings of safety and security in one's neighborhood, incidence of homicide, and risk reports on physical attack, extortion, or robbery." These criteria still tend to focus on the absence of conflict, on the negative, instead of on measuring the presence of conditions that promote peace.

STRATEGIES FOR SUSTAINABLE PEACE

Although basic principles and procedures of mediation and conflict resolution apply to international cases, they present unique challenges. What, then, are the conditions that are essential for promoting peace and for sustaining peaceable relations in the global community of nations?

1. A revised orientation toward resolving international conflict is, as already suggested, urgent; with more attention paid toward promoting sustainable peace, along with ways of preventing conflict. Nations and international organizations are spending billions of dollars reacting to international crises and trying to manage them—military, peacekeeping forces, humanitarian aid, reconstruction programs. These efforts, of course, will continue; but promoting structures of sustainable peace—regional forums for exchange of ideas; joint, regional, and global trade and commerce policies; collaborative peacekeeping forces—are proving themselves to be more affordable and efficient in the long run. Promoting such sustainable peace strategies requires nations to understand not only the causes of conflict but the conditions necessary for peace. In the United States, The Carter Center is developing ways of sustaining peace, not only by fighting poverty, disease, and dictatorial government, but also by providing means for promoting self-sustaining economic practices, improving access to health care, and promoting democratic elections and policies.

2. Organizations like the United Nations and World Court along with NGOs, like Amnesty International and The Carter Center, need to upgrade their financial support and training for quality international mediators and mediation. While the UN already promotes and supports mediation it needs to do so more aggressively. In 2011, the UN General Assembly issued a resolution instructing members to use mediation for the peaceful resolution of conflicts, and it resolved to continue to enhance its own mediation

capabilities, since it already has a Mediation Support Unit. This resolution is an encouraging development, not only because mediation has proven itself capable of resolving conflict, but also because it is uniquely situated to build international relationships and patterns of communication that promote peace and peacemaking into the future.

3. International organizations need to continue to develop research on completed international mediations, both successful and unsuccessful. It is important that rigorous studies be conducted, empirical data collected, and sound theories and models developed in order to better understand not only the causes of conflicts but also the conditions that promote patterns of peace and peacemaking. The great contribution quality mediation offers to international peace lies not simply in resolving immediate conflicts, but in transforming relationships and rooting them in the soil of mutual respect and communication. To discover those causes and constructive conditions requires empirical data and interpretive models that only careful empirical research and analysis can provide.

4. Education is crucial for the future success of mediated, peaceful conflict resolution and for establishing conditions conducive to sustainable peace. Most importantly two populations especially should be targeted for peace education throughout the world—children/youth and military personnel. By educating children, I mean more than training a few peer mediators, as fine as that is, but training all children in peacemaking communication and conflict resolution skills. Throughout the nations of the world there are many such youth education programs; they are considered key to global peacebuilding among cultures and for uniting nations in the future. Education International (EI) is an organization dedicated to the crucial role of building cultures of peace and non-violence throughout the world. In conjunction with UNESCO's charter and the UN's charter, EI promotes "peace, social justice, human rights, democracy, literacy, respect and dignity for all, international solidarity, respect for workers' rights . . . children's rights, equality between men and women, cultural identity and diversity, Indigenous peoples and minorities rights, [and] the preservation of the environment. . . ."[4] There are many other regional and local programs dedicated to educating children in peacebuilding skills and techniques, such as "The Peace and Conflict Education" curriculum in Palestine.

EDUCATING CHILDREN FOR INTERNATIONAL PEACEBUILDING

No doubt, the future success of international mediation is a function of educating children today. Everyday children are trapped in conflicts they do not know how to manage or resolve—teasing, bullying, jealousies, aggression. Helping children manage and resolve conflicts constructively and educating them in skills of communication is essential not only for their own personal well-being but also for future prospects of international peace. There are many organizations undertaking this pedagogical challenge, including The International Child and Youth Care Network. Such programs offer hope for the future; for while conflicts are common, they learn that insults and aggression and violence are not the only and certainly not the best and most efficient ways to deal with conflict. Educating for peacemaking "enable[s] children to respond non-violently to conflict by using the conflict resolution problem-solving process of negotiation, mediation, and consensus decision-making." Not only that, it enables educators "to manage students' behavior without coercion by emphasizing personal responsibility and self-discipline."[5]

This program identifies four common mediation strategies that can be applied in the public schools: Peer Mediation, Mediation Process Curriculum, Peaceable Classroom strategies, and Peaceable School strategies.

Peer Mediation: Acknowledges that involving youth directly in resolving their own conflicts is important not only for personal edification but for actually getting conflicts managed and resolved collaboratively instead of authoritatively by teachers. Before peer mediation, an Albuquerque elementary school reported a rate of 100–150 playground fights a month. After implementing a peer mediation program, the number of fights was reduced to around 10.[6]

Mediation Process Curriculum: Devoting class time to teaching the process of mediating conflicts significantly reduces conflict and school suspensions. Whether class time might consist of a separate mediation course, a distinct mediation curriculum, or a daily lesson, teaching the basic principles of the mediation process, basic communication skills, and problem-solving skills makes a significant difference in student performance. A North Carolina middle school of more than 700 students, for example, reported a 42 percent decrease in in-school suspensions and a 97 percent reduction in out-of-school suspensions.[7]

Peaceable Classroom Strategies: This collaborative approach "integrates conflict resolution" strategies into the curriculum itself and into the daily management of students in a classroom. A curriculum called "Making Choices about Conflict, Security, and Peacemaking" provides a classroom strategy for constructing a curriculum around peacemaking. It incorporates in a curriculum strategies of cooperation, tolerance of diversity, caring, and communication skills.[8]

Peaceable School Strategies: This strategy integrates all three of the above approaches in every classroom and throughout all the activities of the school. "This approach seeks to create schools where conflict resolution has been adopted by every member of the school community, from the crossing guard to the classroom teacher"; from the janitor, to staff and principal. The entire school community commits itself, young and old, to the principles of non-violent constructive conflict resolution. In evaluating such a program in multiethnic school districts in New York City, it was noted that there was a 71 percent decrease in physical violence in the classroom and a 66 percent decrease in name calling and insults. [9]

Educating children and youth throughout the world for peacemaking is crucial to cultivating internationally strategies that preempt violence as a solution and promote strategies of cooperative, peaceful collaboration. The quality of character most essential for successful conflict resolution and peacemaking, both individually and collectively, is compassion. Educating children for compassion is crucial for shifting global dependence on military might and intimidation to dependence on communication skills and peacemaking strategies. Educating for compassion is especially difficult; it requires strengthening not only individual moral character but communal character as well. What educational techniques are conducive to cultivating compassion in children?

Narrative education is crucial to cultivating compassion. How and why so? Why is storytelling such a powerful tool for education in the practice of compassion? An answer lies partly in the fact that narratives provide access to the emotional life of humans and to nurturing emotions conducive to compassion and collaboration. Martha Nussbaum makes this point forcefully when she explains that our moral emotions very often "are not taught to us directly through propositional claims about the world. . . . They are taught above all through stories. Stories express their [emotions] structure and teach us their dynamics. These stories are constructed by others and then taught and learned. But once internalized, they shape the way life looks and feels."[10] But what is it in particular about narratives that inspire and shape habits of compassion? An answer lies in the fact that narratives are a crucial source for activating the imagination. Imagination is crucial to shaping compassion because narratives possess a power to make the characters of a story so alive and human that those who hear or read them engage and live with them; indeed, they enter into and even internalize those experiences. When those narratives are stories of compassion then the child doubly engages her potential for compassion, both by identifying emotionally with characters in the story and by identifying with characters who practice emotions conducive to cultivating compassion.

Apprentice education is also crucial to cultivating habits of compassion. It is rapidly becoming a truism that a teacher teaches moral character as much by doing as by saying. Or conversely, that a student learns moral character and behavior as much by emulation or service learning as by listening. Training by apprenticeship is essential not only for learning mechanical technique and skill but also for learning moral technique and skill. The actual practice of compassion by children alongside parents and mentors nurtures peaceful, non-aggressive patterns of behavior for resolving conflict. Children will imitate parents and teachers practicing tolerance of children who are different, for example; or imitate teachers who get angry at injustice, or who show students how bullying is unacceptable; or who participate alongside students in serving meals to those who are poor.

In short, educating for compassion is indispensable for success in practicing international mediation. Only if societies are willing to educate their children in the practice of compassion is it likely that nations of the world will immediately think of resolving conflicts collaboratively through mediation instead of through intimidation and threats of violence.

INQUIRY AND REFLECTION EXERCISES

1. Access the United Nation's or The Carter Center's web page. Click on their Mediation/Conflict Resolution line and prepare to summarize in class discussion (a) the mediation program offered by the organization, and (b) where/what international mediations they are currently undertaking.

2. Access "The Camp David Accord" entry of Wikipedia, an international conflict mediated by U.S. President Jimmy Carter and his administration. Based on this account, complete a Conflict Grid. You will be reducing many pages to a one page grid.

3. Research one current international conflict and as far as possible complete a Conflict Grid with the details of the conflict, including possible solutions.

4. Inquire of your home school or school district as to the kinds of mediation/conflict resolution strategies and programs that are being implemented; be prepared to report on and summarize them in class.

5. Access the website of The United States Institute of Peace (USIP). Check out some of the education and community programs offered. Identify and describe one program that you find especially interesting and explain why you might want to participate; for example, the Global Peacebuilding Center.

NOTES

1. Laurie Nathan, "Towards a New Era in International Mediation," (London, UK: Policy Directions: Crisis States Research Center, 2010), p. 1.

2. The twenty-two indicators listed by the Index and published by the Institute for Economics and Peace are:

1. Number of external and internal conflicts
2. Number of deaths from organized conflict (external)
3. Number of deaths from organized conflict (internal)
4. Level of organized conflict (internal)
5. Relations with neighboring countries
6. Level of perceived criminality in society
7. Number of refugees and displaced persons as percentage of population
8. Political instability
9. Terrorist activity
10. Political Terror Scale
11. Number of homicides per 100,000 people
12. Level of violent crime
13. Likelihood of violent demonstrations
14. Number of jailed persons per 100,000 people
15. Number of internal security officers and police per 100,000 people
16. Military expenditure as a percentage of GDP
17. Number of armed-services personnel
18. Volume of transfers of major conventional weapons as recipient (imports) per 100,000 people
19. Volume of transfers of major conventional weapons as supplier (exports) per 100,000 people
20. Financial contributions to UN peacekeeping missions
21. Nuclear and heavy weapons capability
22. Ease of access to small arms and light weapons

3. These organizations are the Uppsala Conflict Data Program, The Economic Intelligence Unit, United Nations Survey of Criminal Trends and Operations of Criminal Justice Systems, the International Center for Prison Studies, International

Institute for Strategic Studies, Stockholm International Peace Research Institute Arms Transfer Database, and Bonn International Center for Conversion.

    4. www.ei-ei.org/en/websections/content__detail/5411.

    5. The International Child and Youth Care Network, CYC-ONLINE (March 2006, Issue 86), p. 1.

    6. *Ibid.*, pp. 1–2.

    7. *Ibid.,* p. 3.

    8. *Ibid.,* p. 3.

    9. *Ibid.*, pp. 3–4.

    10. Martha Nussbaum, *Love's Knowledge: Essays on Philosophy and Literature* (New York, NY: Oxford University Press, 1990), p. 287.

11

Role-Play: Guidelines and Cases

GUIDELINES

Role-play is an important part of mediation training. Trainers try to simulate with their students the conditions and character of an actual mediation session. Of course, the spontaneity and uninhibited, impulsive nature of an actual session are difficult to replicate. And yet, re-enacting mediation sessions, in which the trainee simulates at different times the role of a neutral and the role of a disputant, is essential to preparing candidates for certification. The purpose of this chapter is to provide basic guidelines and cases for teams of three to simulate a mediation session. All three team members play the role of neutral and disputant, based on the stages of the model presented in chapters 5 and 6. In preparation for team role-playing, it is usual for the trainer/teacher to role-play a mediation session as a neutral, in order to give students a sense of and confidence in role-playing their own session.

Guidelines for playing the roles of neutral and disputants are as follows; others can be added to these lists.

Guidelines for Mediation Role-Play Teams

1. Students divide into teams of three. Each member plays the role of neutral once and the role of disputant twice.
2. Each neutral selects a case that she/he wants to mediate; no team can mediate the same case twice. This can be a case from the collection included in this chapter, from an online source, or a case created by the student-neutral. The case should be developed with sufficient detail and multiple disputed issues so as to make for an interesting and substantial session.

3. The other two team members determine which of the disputant roles to play.
4. As homework, the team practices on their own time a mock session for each team member in her role as neutral, in preparation for their mediation session in front of the class.
5. Simulated mediation sessions may last about one hour each. The teacher/trainer can determine whether this allows time for caucusing.

Guidelines for Neutrals

1. Each neutral selects a case to mediate, and schedules with teammates a time outside of class to practice role-playing her role as neutral.
2. In front of the class and teacher, and as neutral, you are responsible for implementing the mediation process—facilitating each stage and each step in each stage of a mediation session.
3. As neutral, you are responsible for remaining impartial and for guaranteeing a fair process and agreement.
4. Remember to stay in your role as neutral. Try to re-create a climate that might occur in an actual mediation session.
5. Even though you and your teammates have practiced your case ahead of time, as neutral you are responsible to take notes during the mediation session, just as a neutral would in an actual session. Take notes as an active listener. Your notes should prepare you to fill out a Conflict Grid and to type up a Memorandum of Agreement. After you role-play as neutral you are required to hand in two items, based on your mediated case—(1) a completed Conflict Grid and (2) a completed Memorandum of Agreement form.

Guidelines for Disputants

1. Invest yourself personally and emotionally in the case and role. Play the role as you might imagine it, exhibiting your personality and emotional tendencies.
2. Remember, you are not entertaining an audience, as an actor might; you are playing a role that has no audience. Try to imitate reality.
3. Each disputant is obligated to violate some of the ground rules and ignore good communication practices throughout the session. Provide opportunities for the neutral to enforce rules and enforce proper use of communication skills.
4. For the sake of some spontaneity, each disputant is obligated to add to the selected case one or two NEW, relevant issues or interests, which neither the neutral or other disputants are aware of ahead of time.

Process Evaluation and Skills Assessment

Neutral's Name: _____ Evaluator's Name_____

3=Very Good   2=Good/Satisfactory   1=Needs Improvement   NA=Not Applicable

Process Evaluation

1. Opening Statement: friendly, organized, clear, ground rules, comprehensive. _____

2. Assisted parties in self-awareness of interests, needs, and concerns by
   summarizing clearly and concisely. _____

3. Assisted both parties in understanding the other's point of view (ask each
   party to summarize a little of what the other says, usually during
   clarification or problem-solving stages). _____

4. Guided the mediation process properly through each stage and the steps
   of each stage. _____

5. Remained neutral; treated each party respectfully, equally, and fairly. _____

6. Able to frame and write a fair, clearly worded and proper Agreement. _____

Skills Assessment

Active Listening _____   Reframing _____

"I" Statements _____   Brainstorming _____

Clarifying Questions _____   Common _____
                                      Ground

Proper Conclusion _____   Priority List _____
Verbalized   of Interests

Summarizing _____

Comments Over: Strengths/Improvements

Figure 11.1.   Process Evaluation and Skills Assessment

5. When brainstorming for an agreement, each disputant must disagree with the other before finally finding ways, with the help of the neutral, to come to resolution on several issues/interests.

Guidelines for Observers

Besides training sessions, achieving certification as a neutral always includes two additional requirements: (1) several observations, in which the trainee observes actual mediation sessions conducted by a certified neutral; (2) several co-mediations under the tutelage of a certified neutral. Observing, evaluating, and assessing mediation sessions and skills are a crucial part of training. Those students who are not participating in a mediation session as neutral or disputant are observers and should be actively involved in evaluation and assessment. Evaluation and assessment involve noting both strengths and weaknesses. For each simulated mediation, the form in figure 11.1 is to be completed by observers.

CASES FOR ROLE-PLAY

Case Study: Divorce: Child Support and Property

Sam and Jane have been separated for thirteen months and are divorcing after three years of marriage. They have one child, Amanda, who is sixteen months old. Jane has residential and legal custody of Amanda; they are living with Jane's parents in a basement apartment. Sam has not seen Amanda very much and not on a regular basis. He requested mediation because he now wants to see Amanda on a regular basis and establish a regular pattern of weekly visitation rights and visitation on holidays, birthdays, and summer vacation. Jane is a bit leery of allowing Sam too much visitation. His apartment is in a "transitional" part of town and unstable neighborhood, at least according to Jane. Jane does not like or respect Sam's new girlfriend, Clair, who is a waitress and smokes and intends to move in with Sam. Sam has not paid regular child support, although he has occasionally given Jane some money to buy food and clothes for Amanda. Jane is not working at the time, but wants to go back to school part-time, to be a nurses' aide. Sam has a new job that pays $2,100.00 a month, with health benefits. Jane wants Sam to pay regular child support according to the state's guidelines. Sam and Jane don't have much property between them but Sam continues to make the monthly payments on Jane's car ($198), but wants to stop this payment. Jane has run up a credit card debt of $2,153.00, and wants Sam to pay it off because much of it was money spent on their daughter.

Jane's parents (Amanda's grandparents) don't want anything to do with Sam and don't want him coming around their house. They provide some child care for Amanda but want this to be a temporary arrangement; they think Sam should contribute to paying for child care, as does Jane.

Case Study: Truancy

Beth, a truancy officer for Jefferson High School, has convened a mediation session for Alice (a sophomore) and her single mother, Martha. Alice has missed four days of school this semester and has been late by at least a half an hour nine times. Beth's responsibility is to enforce the school district's regulations: a limit of three absences a term, unless for medical reasons indicated by a doctor's note; and a limit of three tardies. Both parent and student are liable for truancy violations; any student who violates these regulations is subject to dismissal from school, and parents can be legally incarcerated if negligent. Beth's preference is not to punish student or parent but to try to find ways to make sure Martha can guarantee that Alice gets to school regularly and on time.

Martha's employment requires that she leave the house at 7:00 am; the bus Alice is to catch for school arrives a block away at 7:45 am. If Alice misses the bus she has to walk to school or try to find a ride with a friend. Martha wakes Alice up before she leaves for work. There is an alarm clock with a "snooze" button in Alice's bedroom, but she says she never hears it and swears it does not work. Alice's best friend lives nearby and rides the same bus. Alice's father, Joseph, lives four miles away, and works the graveyard shift at the factory and gets off work at 6:30 am. Martha thinks he should come by the house and make sure Alice is up and ready for school. Joseph refused to come to mediation, and told Alice he would cut off her $25 weekly allowance if she continues to miss school, or is late.

Alice likes to stay up late watching late shows on TV and Martha suspects her of drinking, and thinks she may be smoking dope of some sort, but has not yet discovered where she keeps "the good stuff." Alice definitely has a chip on her shoulder and doesn't give a damn about school. Martha thinks Alice should take responsibility for getting herself to school, and refuses to give Alice a call to make sure she's up and getting ready.

Case Study: Landlord and Tenant

Jenny is a twenty-five-year-old mother of three children (ages five, three, and seven months). She has received welfare assistance for two years, and receives food stamps to help make ends meet. She has been separated from her husband (Robert) for a year, but he still comes by and stays with Jenny and visits the kids occasionally, especially when he is short of cash. Four months ago Jenny moved into her current apartment where Juan is her landlord. She paid her rent ($400.00 a month) for the first two months, from welfare monies set aside for food and clothing; but she owes Juan two months' rent. However, the Department of Social Services will not continue sending Jenny her monthly check ($700.00) until Juan signs a verified statement that Jenny is his tenant. Juan has so far refused to sign the verification form because he thinks Jenny will take the rent/welfare money and move elsewhere without paying him the two months' rent she owes him. Jenny also is withholding her money because of a water leak in the kitchen sink that requires she keep the water there turned off, and because the heat in one bedroom is not working.

Not only does Juan want two months back rent, he is also concerned because he has gotten several calls from other tenants complaining about noisy kids and loud music at Jenny's apartment, and he has asked her to keep the kids quiet in the evening, so as not to disturb the neighbors. Juan also has noticed that Robert is sometimes staying at Jenny's apartment for four or five days at a time, in violation of apartment regulations that limit guests to two nights' visitation each week. Both Juan and Jenny have been verbally abusive to each other, with Juan calling Jenny a "slut" and "slimy bitch" and Jenny calling Juan "undocumented" and "illegal"; both threaten the other with a lawsuit.

Case Study: Builder and Client

Sandy hired Fisher Builders to do some renovation on her aging house. Specifically, she wants her back porch repaired and a bathroom with a shower added. The back porch spans the entire back of the house; its steps are rotting as are the pillars holding up its roof. Part of the back porch is to be turned into the space for the bathroom. A friend (Linda) recommended to Sandy that she contract with Fisher Builders to do the work, assuring her that they have a great reputation and do quality work for a decent price. Scott Fisher, the owner of Fisher Builders, agrees to do the job for Sandy even though he already has a full schedule of work; he agrees to do the work for Sandy as a favor to his friend Linda. Sandy and Scott agree on a contract:

- back porch: $1,800 for materials and $1,250 for labor ($3,050);
- bathroom: $4,300 for materials and $2,400 for labor ($6,700).

Estimated time of completion—two weeks. The contract includes the usual clause accommodating "cost overruns," additional unforeseen expenses, including a statement that the builder must discuss such additional costs with the client when he becomes aware of them and before proceeding.

From the beginning Sandy is unhappy with the two construction workers that Scott Fisher assigns to the project. They both smoke and when Sandy comes home from work her house smells foul; in fact, she claims she is allergic to smoke. Sandy starts locking the doors to the house so they cannot smell it up. The workers begin using the bushes in the backyard to relieve themselves, about which the neighbor lady complains. At the end of one week the project is only 1/3 completed, and Sandy believes it is because the two workers are lazy and incompetent. Moreover, Scott Fisher talks to Sandy about the fact that the back porch is in worse shape than he originally thought; there is rot in the foundation which he could not see when he made his original estimate. Scott estimates that the porch will cost an additional $800 in materials and $300 in labor cost. Sandy is furious.

Scott is unhappy with Sandy. Her attitude is nasty and he's doing this as a favor to her because of their mutual friend. After about a week into the project Sandy decided she wanted to change the size of the back porch steps, and make them wider. And then she also wants to add a window in the bathroom which was not in the original contract. The workers told her any changes will increase the cost of the project but Sandy refuses to accept the additional costs. At the end of the first week, Sandy refuses to pay ½ the total cost as agreed to in the contract. Scott pulls his workers off the job and takes all the unused materials with him.

Case Study: College Administration and Plumbers Union

Kool University is a large (27,000 students) 157-year-old institution. Its aging buildings are not in good shape; many were built sixty years ago or more, when using asbestos was common. With the recent national attention on hazardous materials, the university's administration began to investigate the use of asbestos and other hazardous materials in the older buildings. It was discovered that the lining of many of the pipes in the older buildings contained asbestos, a hazardous material that causes mesothelioma and lung cancer. The administration requested that the plumbers, who were university employees, remove the asbestos from the pipes, so it would not be a danger to students, faculty, and staff. The campus plumbers were members of the local plumbers' union; their normal duties did not include working with or removing asbestos or other materials that had the potential to cause serious illnesses, and their contract did not specify one way or the other that they are to handle asbestos.

The plumbers refused to undertake the removal project citing OSHA regulations and endangerment to the health of the workers. The university argued that it is part of their job as university employees and implied in their contract even though not specified. The university promised it would train and equip them adequately. The union argued that it was not in their contract to undertake such work and that the removal should be outsourced to a qualified company. The administration argued that the cost would almost double if the project was outsourced. A representative of the university administration and a representative of the plumbers' union met with a mediator to try to sort out a solution. Both representatives had looked up OSHA regulations regarding asbestos removal.

Case Study: Neighbors Not So Neighborly

Sherry is a graduate student and serious about her studies; she lives in a small house ½ mile from campus. She pretty much stays to herself and studies, when she is not in class or working. She works early as a waitress at a nearby café, and must go to bed early, around 9:00 pm most evenings. Sherry is religious and a regular at Mass on Sunday mornings at 8:00 am. Mark is an undergraduate student who lives next door to Sherry; he loves to host parties and "gets around" on a motorcycle.

Mark has parties on Wednesdays and Saturdays, and sometimes also on Fridays. He seems like a magnet for a good time, and friends take advantage of it whenever they can. Sherry already had talked to Mark about the loudness and lateness of his parties, particularly those on Wednesday nights. It didn't do much good. Recently she called the cops when a Wednesday party went later than midnight. The party stopped and Mark received a "disturbing the peace" warning. Mark had his revenge though; sometimes late before going to bed he would go out and rev up his motorcycle, "just for the fun of it." Late one night some of his party friends painted in red a cross with the word "Bitch," on Sherry's front door. One day Mark's parents were over; they were talking to Mark on the front sidewalk. Sherry yelled out her window at them: "Teach your dumb kid to grow up; else I'll call the cops again." Mark was embarrassed and offended by this. That Saturday Mark and his friends partied late into the night. Sherry called the cops again; they showed up but Mark had already turned down his stereo. No further action was taken. Sherry threatens to bring charges unless Mark agrees to go to mediation, which he does.

Case Study: No More Business as Usual

McPherson International is a U.S. consumer products safety company with seventy-four employees and a strategic plan to expand into additional global markets. They currently serve Canada and Mexico, with plans to enter Brazil, Peru, and Chile in the next year. Catherine is director of a team that is charged with marketing a McPherson product in these countries. The product is an "auto safety kit" which allows small companies and individuals to administer a "consumer safety" test to their own products and so reduce expenses; otherwise they would have to send these products to McPherson or a competitor for a safety check. Catherine's supervisor, Matt, meets with her team weekly to make sure matters are on track; but these meetings are not going well so a neutral was retained to help resolve certain conflicts.

Matt complains that Catherine's team and team members are not performing adequately; not making progress toward getting things planned and ready to go to market on time. He says that they are not taking the project seriously: they are routinely late to meetings and are lazy; many of them don't participate in discussion, and when they do they are critical and negative about it and don't offer constructive comments and suggestions to move the project forward. Matt feels that some members intentionally block action by abstaining when an item comes to a vote and by so doing are in danger of delaying the project. He threatens to kick some members off the team or even get them fired.

Catherine complains that Matt has so alienated her team that little progress can be made toward completing it, until he changes. Team members do not respect him because he does not seem to respect them. He shouts at them, and he sometimes uses derogatory names when speaking about them; the team feels that Matt generally treats them paternalistically and not as professionals. Furthermore, Matt is in the habit of altering the minutes of meetings to suit himself and without consulting the committee before doing so and before distributing them. Also team members complain that Matt schedules the meetings when it is convenient for himself and not convenient for the team. He schedules meetings at 7:00 am, his routine time of arrival; whereas team members typically do not begin their work day until 8:00 am. Team members have threatened to write a damning letter to Matt's boss if things don't change; some have threatened to resign from the team.

References

Arbinger Institute. *Leadership and Self-Deception: Resolving the Heart of Conflict*, Second Edition. Oakland, CA: Berrett-Koehler Pub. (2002).

———. *The Anatomy of Peace*. Oakland, CA: Berrett-Koehler Pub. (2008).

Beer, Jenifer E., Packard, Caroline C., Stief, Eileen. *The Mediator's Handbook: Revised and Expanded Fourth Edition*. Gabriola Island, BC, Canada: New Society Pub. (2012).

Braithwaite, John. *Restorative Justice and Responsive Regulation*. London, UK: Oxford University Press (2002).

Bush, Robert and Folger, Joseph. *The Promise of Mediation: The Transformative Approach to Mediation*, New York, NY: Jossey-Bass Pub. (2004).

Fisher, Roger and Shapiro, D. *Beyond Reason: Using Emotions as You Negotiate*. New York: Viking Press (2005).

Fisher, Roger and Ury, William, *Getting to Yes: Negotiating Agreement Without Giving In*. New York: Penguin Books (1981/2011).

Florenza, Samuel, "Mediation and Psychotherapy: Parallel Processes," in *Community Mediation: A Handbook for Practitioners and Researchers*, eds. Karen Duffy, James Grosch, Paul Olczak. New York: The Guilford Press (1991).

Kinsey, William D., et al., *Mediator Communication Competencies: Problem Solving and Transformative Practices*, Fifth Edition. Boston, MA: Pearson Custom Pub. (2005).

Lechman, Barbara A. Nagel, *Conflict and Resolution*, Second Edition. New York: Wolters Kluwer, Aspen Pub. (2008).

Lederach, John Paul. *Building Peace: Sustainable Reconciliation in Divided Societies*. Washington, DC: United States Institute of Peace (1998).

Nathan, Laurie, *Towards a New Era in International Mediation*. London, UK: Policy Directions: Crisis States Research Center (2010).

Nussbaum, Martha. *Love's Knowledge: Essays on Philosophy and Literature*. New York: Oxford University Press (1990).

Walgrave, Lode. *Restorative Justice, Self-Interest and Responsible Citizenship.* Cillompton, Devon, UK: Willan Pub. (2008).

Woolford, Andrew. *The Politics of Restorative Justice: A Critical Introduction.* Halifax and Winnipeg: Fenwood Pub. (2009).

Zehr, Howard, *The Little Book of Restorative Justice.* New York, NY: Skyhorse Pub. (2015).

Index

About the Author

James E. Gilman is professor emeritus of philosophy and religion at Mary Baldwin University in Staunton, Virginia. He has been a volunteer mediator with The Fairfield Center in Harrisonburg, Virginia and is currently a mediator trainer at The Whatcom Dispute Resolution Center in Bellingham, Washington. For many years he taught a college course titled "Mediation: Theory and Practice" and has taught workshops in conflict resolution for community organizations and for churches. His previous books include *Fidelity of Heart: An Ethic of Christian Virtue*; *Christian Faith, Reason and Compassion: A Philosophy of the Christian Faith*; and *Christian Faith, Justice and a Politics of Mercy: The Benevolent Community*.

CPSIA information can be obtained
at www.ICGtesting.com
Printed in the USA
BVOW08*1937161216

R7719900001B/R77199PG470016BVX1B/1/P